The Winning Leadership Challenge

The Winning Leadership Challenge

An Eight-Step Challenge for Students to Empower the Winning Leader Within

Kelly Simmons III

The Winning Leadership Challenge
An Eight-Step Challenge for Students to Empower the Winning
Leader Within

Disclaimer: This book has been published for the purpose of
providing the reader with general information on its subject matter.
The author and the publisher believe the information to be accurate
and authoritative at the time of publication. The book is sold with the
understanding that neither the author nor the publisher is providing
professional advice, and the reader should not rely upon this book as
such. Every situation is different, and professional advice (whether
psychological, legal, financial, tax, or otherwise) should only be
obtained from a professional licensed in your jurisdiction who has
knowledge of the specific facts and circumstances.

Cover Design by Katie Fleming
Interior Layout and Design by Alice Briggs
Editorial Team: Cindy McCachern , Chloie Benton, Ginny Glass,
Proofreader

ISBNs:
Ebook: 979-8-89165-240-8
Paperback: 979-8-89165-238-5
Hardcover: 979-8-89165-239-2

Published by:
Streamline Books
Kansas City, MO
www.streamlinebookspublishing.com

To My Family

I dedicate this book to the entire Simmons and Robinson Family. To my loving wife, Kelley, and our children—Orren, Jayce, Zakee, and Lisa—and to our granddaughter, Ziamara. Thank you for your support and for being my number one fans. Keep winning! I am also grateful to my grandparents, aunts, uncles, nieces, nephews, and cousins for their continuous support and encouragement throughout my life.

To my father, Kelly Simmons Jr., and my mother, the late Gladys Simmons, thank you for being my first and most inspiring examples of servant leadership and for teaching me the value of character, hard work, and excellence. I am who I am today because of you, and I love you both dearly.

To my father and mother-in-law, Marion and Gloria Robinson, thank you for your steadfast love and support. To my sisters—Vickie, Jean, Jackie, and Gwen—thank you for your unwavering love and protection of your "Big Baby Brother." To my sisters-in-law—Tia, April, and Melanie— thank you for your kindness and for allowing me to be your big brother. To my brothers-in-law—Ken Rogers, Gary Scott, Bobby Walker, and Theolander Wilson—thank you for being mighty men in every sense of the word. Finally, to my pastor, Pastor Henry Simons, his lovely wife, Kimberly Simons, and my entire church family at Truth Church and Ministries, thank you so much for your love and support over the years. I love you always!

To My Mentors and Coaches, Past and Present

Dr. Carl Wells, Pastor Ron Moss, Pastor Demetric Middleton, Roland & Maleia Wilson Sr., Dallas Webb, the late Rosa Boseman, Ron and Linda Harvey, Pam Green, Dr. Antwon Sutton, Michael Donald, Charlie Boseman, David Lee Harrison Sr., Pastor Darryl Hall, Marcus Scott, Dr. Robert Kirton, Leroy Garrison, Stan Wardlaw, Pastor Wendell Jones, David Sturgeon, Pastor Thomas Davis, Anthony Bryant, Ricky Taylor, Dr. Sherry Rivers, Pastor William H. Cox, Audrey Breland, Michael Donald, Elaine Billie, Larry Thorne Sr., JacQuie Parmlee-Bates, Milton & Melissa Smith, Pastor Moises Rivera, Troy Thames, Dr. Kaye Shaw, Bency Beals, Jamar Washington Sr., Horace Alexander, Tom Ledbetter, Douglas Lineberry, LeMont Acox, Stan Johnson, and the late Pastor Andrew D. Jones and Denise Jones: thank you for pouring into my life and challenging me to grow. Each of you has played a significant part in my life, career, business, and personal journey. I am forever grateful.

To My Dear Friend

I also dedicate this work to my dear friend, the late Donald "Donnie" Owen Ridlehuber, Founder of Openhands Outreach Camp in Greenwood, South Carolina. Donnie's genuine love for serving young people and those less fortunate continues to inspire me, his family and friends. Your legacy lives on!

To My Former and Current Students

Thank you for encouraging me to write this book and for all you have taught me over the past fifteen years—through every classroom, workshop, counseling session, pep rally, and service-learning project. I am truly grateful for your impact on my life.

To My Readers

Thank you for supporting me by reading and purchasing this book. If someone gave it to you, be sure to thank them. I hope you take notes, put each winning leadership step into practice, and discover your own path to success. If this book impacts your life, please consider sharing your experience by leaving a positive review on Amazon. Your feedback helps spread the message of The Winning Leadership Challenge far and wide.

CONTENTS

INTRODUCTION

Hey, winning leader! Coach Kelly here.

Are you ready to step into the world of leadership? Perhaps you think leaders are only the loud, confident ones—the athletes, the influencers, or the people who always seem to have everything figured out. But I've got a secret for you: you're a leader too! That's right, even if you don't see it yet. I'm here to coach, guide, and help you uncover the winning leader already inside you.

In this book, I'll take you through my **Eight Winning Leadership Steps** to help you become the leader you were always meant to be. Leadership isn't reserved for a particular group of people—it's something we all can grow into. And my job? I'm here to help you on that journey, coach you through each step, and give you the tools you need to succeed.

So, Why Am I Writing This Book?

As a career counselor and leadership coach, I've worked with many students like you. Students who may or may not see themselves as leaders and were struggling to find their way or didn't have the confidence to step up.

And every single time, I've seen them transform. They've discovered talents they didn't know they had. They've learned how to speak up for themselves, prepare for their futures, and become successful adults. That's what I want for you too.

I'm not just here to give you tips on being a good student. I'm here to help you recognize your power, guide you as you build confidence, and show you how to become a winning leader no matter who you are.

What Qualifies Me to Be Your Coach?

I've been in your shoes. I was a first-generation college graduate who had no idea how to navigate the world of school, careers, or leadership. I faced many challenges, but I didn't let them stop me. I went on to become an officer in the US Army and a corporate sales leader, and now, I've spent over fifteen years working with middle, high school, and college students to help them find their path to success. I didn't start out seeing myself as a leader, but along the way, I learned that leadership is more than being the loudest or most popular person in the room. It's about understanding that leadership impacts everything we do.

Why Is This Book Important to You?

As a teenager or young adult today, you face more challenges than ever, figuring out who you are, what you want to do, and how you fit into the world. All of this can feel overwhelming. Social media tells you to look, talk, and act a certain way. Sometimes, it feels like you'll never measure up. You may doubt yourself, feel like you don't belong, or struggle to find your voice. But I'm here to tell you that you belong, you have a voice, and you are enough.

You might be comparing yourself to what you see on-line, thinking, "I'm not as dope, outgoing, or successful as them," or "I don't have what it takes." But you do have what it takes. You need to see it, own it, and grow into it. You don't need to be the show's star or have straight A's to be a leader. You need to start right where you are and build on what you already have.

What Is Leadership Anyway?

When we think about leadership, we often think about people we admire—maybe your favorite social media in-fluencer, an athlete, a teacher, your parents or someone in your community. But leadership isn't just about being in charge or getting attention. Leadership starts with you—serving others, connecting with people, and making an impact. It's about inviting people on a journey with you, not forcing them to follow.

That's what I'm going to help you do in this book. I'll teach you how to discover and develop your leadership style, learn from your failures, communicate your vision, and lead confidently—whether in your school, community, family, or career.

My Leadership Journey: From Struggles to Success

I didn't always see myself as a leader. I used to think leaders were dictators who always told others what to do, and I didn't want that responsibility. But as I got older, my view of leadership changed. I realized that leadership isn't about controlling people. Instead, it's about being myself, accepting responsibility, serving people, and helping them reach their goals. It's about using my gifts, talents, and skills to make an impact in the world.

Like you, I didn't always have it figured out. I wasn't always confident. I faced struggles and setbacks that made me doubt my abilities. But I learned that every challenge was a chance to grow over time. I knew that leadership started with believing in myself, and that's what I want to help you do.

What Does Coach Kelly's Winning Leadership Look Like?

Winning leadership is about discovering the leader within you to serve, connect, direct, and influence yourself and others to reach a desired outcome that has a meaningful impact. Imagine leadership as an interstate, a roadway connecting people to where they want to go and offering direction. As drivers travel, they encounter billboards and road signs pointing them toward gas stations, restaurants, scenic spots, or resting places. These signs influence their decisions by encouraging them to take the next exit to fill up their vehicles, grab a meal, stretch their legs, or take a break. Like these roads, a winning leader serves, connects, directs, and influences people toward a desired outcome.

As a winning leader, you're not just focused on reaching your own destination—you're also helping others get to theirs. The connections you make, the guidance you provide, and the influence you have will help others achieve their goals. Throughout this book, I'll show you how your leadership can make a lasting impact, not just in your own life but in the lives of those around you, whether it's helping a friend, leading a team, or taking the next step toward your dream career, your leadership matters. I'm here to coach you through each step of the journey.

You Were Born to Be A Winning Leader!

Are you ready to take the next step in your journey? You might be in middle school, high school, or even college, wondering what your next step should be. But no matter where you are, I want you to know you have what it takes to succeed. It all starts with your leadership.

In this book, I'll share my **Eight Winning Leadership Steps** to help you become the winning leader you were born to be. You don't need perfect grades, a million social media followers, or a huge bank account to lead. All you need is faith in yourself and the determination to work hard. Are you ready to accept **The Winning Leadership Challenge**?

I'm so proud of you for picking up this book and starting your leadership journey. You've already taken the first step. Now, let's keep going—**one step at a time**. Let's win together!

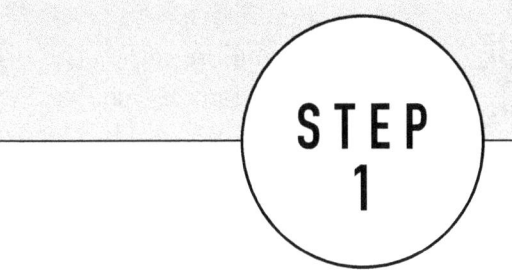

STEP 1

Discover the Winning Leader in You

Winning leadership is for everyone, not just for those with a title or position!

You Were Born to Win!

Let's start with a big question: Are leaders born or made? People have debated this for years, but here's a fun fact: research says leadership is 70 percent learned and only 30 percent genetic. That means most of us become leaders through our experiences and choices. So, guess what? You have the potential to be a winning leader!

THERE IS A LEADER INSIDE YOU WAITING TO BE DISCOVERED.

But first, what comes to mind when you think of a leader? Maybe you imagine someone like a coach, your favorite music artist, or even a teacher. It's easy to see leadership as belonging to the big names, the "famous" people. But here's the truth: There is a leader inside *you* waiting to be discovered.

The Real Meaning of Leadership

Before we dive in, let's clear up something important. Leadership isn't just about being in charge or telling people what to do. It's about making an impact. As I mentioned before, it's about serving, connecting, directing, and influencing others to reach a desired outcome that has a meaningful impact. You don't need to be the student body president, a star athlete, or a straight-A student to do that.

You might be thinking, "How do I even start?" Great question! This winning leadership challenge is all about discovering who you are as a leader and your unique leadership style, and I'm here to help you every step of the way.

Meet Coach Kelly's Six Winning Leadership Styles

You might not know this, but there are different types of leaders. Each of them is uniquely different. Think of these winning leadership styles as "superpowers." Which one sounds like you?

1. **The Observer**: You're the person who always notices what's going on. You're introverted, detailed, self-aware, and good at guiding your friends when they need help. You have that talent to pick up the little things that others miss.

2. **The Protector**: You hate confusion and chaos. You're the one who stands up for others and keeps things running smoothly. If your friend is in trouble, you're the first to have their back.

3. **The Connector:** You love meeting new people and bringing them together. You're the social butterfly who's great at getting everyone talking. You know how to make people feel included, valued, and a part of the team.

4. **The Influencer:** You're the go-to person in your group. People trust your advice because you've got that "it" factor. Whether sharing your experiences or being really good at something, others naturally look to you for guidance. You have what it takes to lead the way.

5. **The Director:** You like to take charge. You have a clear vision and know how to organize your crew to make things happen. You ensure everyone knows what to do when there's a group project. You have a way to share the vision and focus on priorities.

6. **The Server:** You're all about helping others. You're dependable, always willing to lend a hand, and put others first. You're the friend who's always there when others need you—the one people can count on. You inspire everyone around you to serve and make a difference.

Remember: All of these styles are winning leadership styles! There's no "one right way" to be a leader. The world needs all kinds of winning leaders, including you.

My Journey: From Shy Kid to Leader

Let me share a bit more about myself. Growing up in Anderson, South Carolina, I didn't see myself as a leader. I was the quiet kid who sat in the classroom and tried to stay out of the spotlight. I didn't want to stand out or draw attention to myself. I wasn't super popular or the best at anything—I was trying to blend in.

Honestly, I didn't try very hard. I'd get C's and D's in school, and deep down, I knew I had the potential to make A's and B's, but I was afraid of putting in the effort and failing. I didn't believe in myself, and I felt like being a leader was something other people did—not me. I felt unconfident and thought, *Why even bother trying if I'm just going to mess up?*

But here's the thing: even though I didn't see myself as a leader, I had incredible leadership examples right before me. Even though neither graduated from college, my dad was a pastor, and my mom was a stay-at-home mom who ran a little side business. Dad went to the Army and a technical school to become an air conditioning technician. Later, when he was called into ministry to be a pastor, he studied and earned a certificate in theology from Erskine College in Due West, South Carolina. My mom, who left school in the tenth grade because she had to work, built a successful flea marketing business from the ground up. I believe I inherited my entrepreneurial spirit from her and my love of people from them both.

My parents worked hard, set powerful examples for me and my sisters, and taught me the value of serving others. I learned so much from them about respect, dedication, sacrifice, and helping those around me. Still, despite their influence, I didn't see myself as someone who could be a leader.

I did have some early influences, though. As a kid, I joined Cub Scouts and continued into Boy Scouts. My Scout leaders had a profound influence on me as I grew older, teaching me the value of teamwork, responsibility, and serving others. They showed me what it meant to be a leader, but I still didn't think I could be one. I always felt like I was just one of the followers, not someone who could step up and lead.

Then, in the eighth grade, my parents decided to let me play football. Now, let me tell you, I was pretty good. I scored several touchdowns and made some game-winning plays. But joining the football team was a turning point for me. For the first time, I experienced what being part of a team meant, and I realized that every role mattered. That's when I started to understand that leadership isn't always about being in the spotlight—sometimes, it's about being a part of a community beyond yourself to follow, add value, and encourage others.

Things changed even more when I joined the Navy Junior ROTC program my freshman year at T. L. Hanna High School in Anderson, South Carolina. It was a completely new environment for me. For the first time, my instructors and senior cadets began to tell me, "Hey, there's a leader in you." At first, I didn't believe them. How could I be a leader when I didn't even have confidence in myself? But then something amazing happened—they gave me leadership roles and responsibilities. They trusted me to take charge of tasks, organize events, and even guide other students.

It was terrifying at first. I remember once, my NJROTC unit was preparing for a big drill competition. I was tasked with organizing a team practice. I kept thinking, "What if I mess this up? What if they don't listen to me?" But I pushed through those doubts, and we ended up doing well. That moment made me realize that maybe, just maybe, I had what it took to be a leader.

But it still wasn't easy. Even though I was in leadership roles, I didn't always believe in myself. Sometimes, I felt like an imposter, like I was pretending to be something I wasn't. Each time I stepped up, I learned something new about myself. I realized I could handle responsibility, that people were willing to listen, and that my ideas mattered. Bit by bit, I started to build my confidence.

A Defining Moment: The Mr. T. L. Hanna Pageant

One of my most defining moments happened during my senior year of high school. I decided to do something entirely out of my comfort zone—I entered the Mr. T. L. Hanna Pageant. Now, this was a big deal. The pageant was a yearly competition at my high school to recognize an exemplary senior boy. Community leaders judged contestants on their interview skills, talent, and appearance in both casual and formal wear.

I remember talking to some of my football teammates about entering the pageant. We joked about it, saying, "How hard could it be?" I was a pretty good dancer back then, and when my best friend Cedric decided to enter, I thought, *Why not? Let's have some fun.*

But as the competition approached, I started to take it more seriously. I rented a tuxedo, practiced my dance moves, and worked on my public speaking skills. On the night of the pageant, I felt excited and nervous. Part of me was convinced I could not win, but another part was proud of myself just for trying.

I couldn't believe it when the winners were announced—they called my name. At first, I thought it was a mistake. Me? The winner? But it was real. And not only did I win, but I also became the first African American to win the pageant. That moment changed everything for me. It was the first time I felt like I could be more than what I had always thought I was. It made me realize that amazing things can happen when I step out of my comfort zone.

The Power of Stepping Out of Your Comfort Zone

If I could go back and give my younger self some advice, I'd say, "Take the mental limits off and take more risks. Don't be afraid to try new things, even if they scare you." That pageant taught me that people grow the most when they're willing to challenge themselves and face their fears. While it's easy to stay in your comfort zone, nothing great happens there.

Going to College: A Turning Point

A huge turning point came when I graduated high school and went to college. No one in my family had ever earned a college degree at the time, so this was uncharted territory. I didn't have a clear path; honestly, I felt like I didn't belong. I'd spent years doubting myself, so taking that step into college was a huge deal. But deep down, I knew I wanted to challenge myself and improve.

After my first semester at Charleston Southern University, my grade point average plummeted to 1.7. It was a wake up call that I needed to change my study habits and approach to school. Determined to turn things around, I transferred to Lander University in Greenwood, South

Carolina, where I joined the Army ROTC program and got involved in several different student organizations. I decided to throw myself into these opportunities, even though I was nervous and unsure. That's when something incredible happened—people started to take notice. They saw potential in me that I hadn't yet recognized in myself, which made all the difference.

I remember the day I was elected president of a student organization on campus—it felt surreal. Once the quiet kid who sat in class hoping no one would notice me, I was now standing in front of my peers as their leader. And you know what? I loved it. I enjoyed bringing people together, setting goals, and seeing everyone work toward a common purpose. It was the first time in my life that I felt like I was making a difference, and it felt amazing.

This newfound confidence grew even more when I became a presidential ambassador at the university. Suddenly, I represented my university at events, led campus tours, met new people, and spoke in large groups on behalf of the president. Whenever someone said, "You're a great leader," I could feel another layer of self-doubt peel away. It was like puzzle pieces coming together, forming a clearer picture of the person I was meant to be.

My most significant turning point was learning to stop comparing myself to others. For so long, I had convinced myself that I didn't fit the "leader" mold because I wasn't

> LEADERSHIP IS ABOUT BEING WILLING TO SERVE, SUPPORT, AND GUIDE OTHERS.

the smartest, the loudest, or the most popular. But I began to realize that leadership comes in many forms. It's not about just being the most extroverted person in the room. Instead, leadership is about being willing to serve, support, and guide others. That realization allowed me to embrace myself instead of trying to be someone I wasn't.

After college, I took on even more significant leadership roles when I joined the military as a commissioned officer. This was another level of responsibility, pushing me to keep growing and developing my skills. But this time, instead of doubting myself, I embraced the challenge. I saw every obstacle as an opportunity to learn and become a better leader. I realized that leadership wasn't about having all the answers but learning, adapting, and always trying to improve.

College: Pushing My Limits

College was my chance to push my limits and redefine myself. I challenged myself to be more courageous, outgoing, and confident. I started to see that leadership wasn't about being perfect but about being willing to learn, make mistakes, and keep going.

One of the most important things I learned was the power of listening. As I took on more leadership roles, I realized that being a great leader isn't about always being the one talking or making all the decisions. It's about listening to others, valuing their opinions, and creating an environment where everyone feels heard and respected. That's when I truly started to understand the impact I could have on others.

Embracing the Challenges

One of the most challenging but rewarding things I did was embrace the challenges that came my way. There were times when I doubted myself, failed, and felt overwhelmed. But I learned that every challenge was an opportunity to grow. Instead of letting those moments break me, I let them build me.

When I graduated from college and became a commissioned officer in the military, I again faced new challenges. I had to make tough decisions, lead a team, and earn the respect of those around me. But I realized that every experience—feeling scared or confident—shaped me into the leader I was meant to be.

Believing in Myself and Others

Looking back, I realize my greatest breakthrough happened when I learned to believe in myself—and not just in myself, but in the people around me as well. As I gained more confidence, I started to see how powerful it was to encourage others, lift them, and help them see their potential. That's when I truly understood that leadership isn't about being at the top but helping others rise.

LEADERSHIP IS ABOUT BEING BRAVE ENOUGH TO SEARCH WITHIN AND TRY, STRONG ENOUGH TO KEEP GOING, AND KIND ENOUGH TO HELP OTHERS.

If I could sum up my journey in one lesson, it would be this: Leadership isn't about being perfect or having all the answers. It's about being brave enough to search within and try, strong enough to keep going, and kind enough to help others.

||||||||||||||||||||||||||||||||||||||||||||||||||||||||||||||||||||||||||||||||||||||||

Coaching Tip: Challenge yourself to take that first step and get out of your comfort zone. Don't be scared to believe in yourself, even when it feels like no one else does. Because the truth is, that's where authentic leadership begins—with you.

||||||||||||||||||||||||||||||||||||||||||||||||||||||||||||||||||||||||||||||||||||||||

Discover Your Winning Leadership Style

You might wonder, *Why should I even care about my leadership style?* Well, here's the deal—knowing your leadership style isn't just about figuring out how to boss people around or be in charge. It's about understanding your strengths, how you interact with others, and how you can make a real impact in the world around you right now.

When you hear "leadership," what pops into your mind? Maybe it's the captain of your school's basketball team, the student council president, or even your favorite YouTuber. But guess what? You're already showing leadership in your way, even if you don't realize it yet.

You're a leader when you do any of the following:

- Help your friend who's struggling with assignments instead of letting them give up.
- Step up and take charge of a group project when no one else wants to lead.
- Stand up for yourself or someone being mistreated, even if it feels awkward.
- Organize a gaming night with friends or start a club because you see a need.
- Doing the right things when nobody is watching.

Leadership isn't just a title—it's an action word. It's about showing up, being there for others, and doing the right thing, even when it's tough. And here's the best part: there's no single "right" way to be a leader. That's why we want you to discover your unique style.

||||||||||||||||||||||||||||||||||||||||||||||||||||||||||||||||||||||||||||||||||

Coaching Tip: Challenge yourself by taking the Winning Leadership Style quiz. It will help you discover more about your strengths as a leader.

||||||||||||||||||||||||||||||||||||||||||||||||||||||||||||||||||||||||||||||||||

DISCOVER YOUR WINNING LEADERSHIP STYLE QUIZ

So, are you ready to discover the leader in you? Let's do this! This quiz is super simple—no grades, no pressure, just a way to understand yourself better. Answer honestly, and don't overthink it. The goal here is to help you recognize the kind of leader you are right now and the leader you're becoming. Remember, there's no "perfect" style—only *your* style.

Ready? Let's Go!

Question 1
When working on a group project, you find yourself doing one of the following:

    A) Observing the team's progress and providing helpful suggestions when needed.

    B) Ensuring everyone is comfortable and no one is confused about their roles.

    C) Connecting with everyone and making sure communication is flowing well.

    D) Motivating the team by sharing your knowledge and experience.

    E) Taking charge, organizing tasks, and ensuring the project stays on track.

    F) Offering help and support to team members who need assistance.

Question 2

When faced with a difficult decision, you usually do one of these:

    A) Analyze all the details and consider the impact on everyone involved.

    B) Think about how to protect yourself and others from any adverse outcomes.

    C) Reach out to others to discuss options and gather different perspectives.

    D) Trust your instincts and lead, knowing others will follow.

    E) Set a clear direction and guide others toward the best solution.

    F) Consider how you can best support those affected by the decision.

Question 3

If you see a friend struggling with a problem, you are most likely to do one of the following:

    A) Observe quietly, waiting for the right moment to offer helpful advice.

    B) Step in to protect them and ensure they feel safe and supported.

    C) Introduce them to others who can help and encourage them to connect with more resources.

    D) Share your experiences to inspire and help them see a way forward.

    E) Take charge of the situation and provide them with a plan of action.

    F) Offer your assistance and be there for them every step of the way.

Question 4

In a team setting, you prefer to do one of these:

A) Pay attention to everyone's strengths and weaknesses to help guide the team.

B) Ensure that the team's environment is positive and conflict-free.

C) Build relationships with team members and encourage collaboration.

D) Take the lead and inspire others with your ideas and vision.

E) Assign tasks, set goals, and keep the team focused on the result.

F) Support your teammates by helping with tasks and ensuring everyone feels valued.

Question 5

When given a new challenge, your first instinct is to:

A) Gather as much information as possible and analyze all the details.

B) Ensure that you and others are protected from potential risks.

C) Discuss the challenge with others to gather different ideas and solutions.

D) Step up and lead the way, showing confidence and enthusiasm.

E) Create a plan, delegate tasks, and organize a path to success.

F) Offer your assistance to anyone needing help with the challenge.

Question 6

You feel most fulfilled as a leader when you do one of the following:

A) Notice how your insights helped improve the team's performance.

B) Know that everyone feels safe, valued, and understood.

C) See people connecting and building strong relationships because of your efforts.

D) Realize that others trust and follow your guidance.

E) Achieve a goal together due to your leadership and organization.

F) Witness the success of others that you supported and helped along the way.

Question 7

When you see someone making a mistake, you are most likely to:

A) Point it out gently, offering suggestions on how to improve.

B) Step in to help them avoid making the same mistake again.

C) Encourage them to talk about what happened and offer your support.

D) Share a story of overcoming a similar mistake and offer guidance.

E) Give clear instructions on how to correct the mistake and prevent it from happening again.

F) Help them fix the mistake and reassure them that it's okay.

Scoring Your Quiz

For each answer you chose, assign yourself one point for the corresponding leadership style.

- **A = Observer**
- **B = Protector**
- **C = Connector**
- **D = Influencer**
- **E = Director**
- **F = Server**

Add up the total points for each winning leadership style. The style with the highest score reflects your dominant leadership style, while other styles with higher scores indicate your secondary strengths.

Once you've tallied your points, you'll see which winning leadership style fits you best. Don't be surprised if you match more than one style—that's normal! Most of us have a mix of different leadership styles and strengths.

So, What's Next?

By taking this quiz, you've taken the first step in discovering your winning leadership style. Whether you're an observer who notices all the details or a server who's always there to help others, your style makes you unique. Embrace it, own it, and use your strengths to make a difference.

Remember: You don't need a title or a fancy role to be a leader. You need to be yourself, and that's more than enough.

The Power of Your Story

Every winning leader has a story, and your story is powerful. Think about the moments in your life that have shaped you—the challenges you've faced, the people who've inspired you, and the times you've stepped up for others. These experiences are what make your leadership style unique. Your story matters, and it's what makes you a fantastic leader.

Let's Wrap It Up: Winning Leadership Begins with You

You don't need to be the most popular or the most intelligent student to be a leader. All you need is the willingness to grow, learn, and make a difference. As you read this book, I want you to remember one thing: You've got this! You have the potential to be a winning leader, and I'm so excited to help you discover that winning leader within you.

Are you ready to start this journey? Let's go, leader—it's time to win!

Winning Leadership in Action

1. Get together with some friends and grab a giant poster board. Divide it into six sections and label each with a leadership style: observer, protector, connector, influencer, director, and server. At the top of your poster, write down a real issue students face, such as bullying, loneliness, or peer

pressure. Then, in each section, draw or doodle a picture that shows how that leadership style would handle the problem. Make it fun and creative! Once you're done, choose someone from your group to present your poster and explain your ideas. Talk about how each leadership style brings something unique to solving problems and why having different kinds of leaders working together is essential.

2. Take a sheet of paper and draw a timeline of your life. Think back to several moments when you stepped up as a leader. Don't worry—these don't have to be huge! Maybe it was when you stood up for someone, organized a fun hangout, or helped a teammate during a game. Get creative—add some doodles, colors, or symbols that represent those moments. Once you're done, pair up with a friend and trade timelines. Then, talk about your leadership moments and what they meant to you.

3. Create a collage with images, quotes, words, or drawings representing leaders you admire. These can be people you know personally (like teachers, family members, or friends) or public figures (like athletes, activists, musicians, or historical figures). Feel free to bring in pictures or create drawings to add to your collage. What qualities make these individuals great leaders? Do you see any leadership styles (observer, protector, connector, influencer, director, server) in your role models?

4. Think of one leadership quality from this chapter that you want to work on this week. Do you want

to be a better listener, like an observer, or stand up for a friend like a protector? Next week, be ready to share how you applied that leadership quality to your life. What did you learn about yourself?

Looking back on this step, what do you consider your most valuable takeaway? Write your answer below:

_____

_____

_____

_____

_____

_____

_____

_____

_____

_____

_____

_____

_____

_____

_____

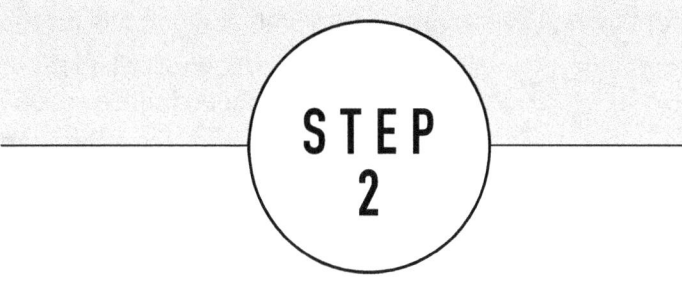

Learn How to Fail Forward

The key to winning in life is learning from your failures, starting again, and not hitting repeat!

Your Leadership Journey

Now that you've discovered your winning leadership style, let's take a closer look at what makes each style unique. Remember: most people aren't just one type of leader. While you may identify strongly with one style, you likely have elements of other leadership styles. As you grow and learn, you'll have the opportunity to develop strengths from all styles, creating a well-rounded and practical approach to leadership.

Embracing Failure as Part of the Journey

When you think about winning, losing may be the last thing that comes to mind. It's easy to focus on the victories, the moments when everything goes right, and you feel on top of the world. But the truth is, all great leaders have faced failure—probably more times than they can count. Here's the thing: it's not about how many times you fall but how many times you get back up.

IT'S NOT ABOUT HOW MANY TIMES YOU FALL BUT HOW MANY TIMES YOU GET BACK UP.

You might wonder, *Why would I want to focus on failure?* That's because learning how to lose is a vital part of your growth as a leader. When you embrace failure as an opportunity to learn, you understand that every setback is a setup for a comeback. Remember: failure is never final!

My Story from Struggles to Strength

School was always a challenge for me. I wasn't that kid who had it all figured out or effortlessly got straight A's. I was the complete opposite. I did just enough to get by—nothing more, nothing less. And because of that, I started to believe that I didn't have what it took to succeed. I began to think, *Maybe I'm just not cut out for this.*

Some of my classmates didn't care much about school, so I fit in with them. We were the group that never got labeled as "gifted" or "honors"—just the regular kids in general classes. Looking back, I'd probably be called an "at-risk" student today. I wasn't a troublemaker; I was just a good kid who struggled with academics and confidence. But deep down, I felt like I was constantly swimming upstream, and no matter how hard I tried, I couldn't keep up.

The truth is school took effort—something I wasn't used to putting in. Everything about it was hard for me—tests, homework, and reading assignments felt like climbing a mountain. I'd read something, but it wouldn't stick. I had to go over it repeatedly to make sense of it, and even then, I'd often fail. Each failure chipped away at my confidence a little more. I never talked to my teachers or friends about it because I didn't want them to know how much I struggled. I guess I thought I was supposed to figure it out on my own.

As the years passed, I developed a pattern—do just enough to get by. I didn't want to stand out, whether for being great or being the kid who failed. But even when I failed, my teachers gave me opportunities to make up the work, and I always took them. I didn't want to be left behind. That kept me moving forward—the fear of getting stuck while everyone else moved on.

About every year while in middle school, I found myself back in summer school. I wouldn't say I liked it, but it was my lifeline. With the extra attention and support, I managed to make up my grades, but once the summer ended, I'd return to just getting by. I never found the drive to work harder during the school year, and it became a vicious cycle. Because I knew I wasn't doing my best, I always felt I was cheating myself.

The worst part was that I started to believe the lie that I wasn't smart enough. I'd see my classmates breeze through assignments while I struggled and think, *Maybe this just isn't for me.* There were even times when I felt so overwhelmed that I cheated on tests. I'd peek at the answers of the person next to me, hoping to pass without getting caught. But every time I cheated, I felt even smaller, like I was proving to myself that I couldn't do it on my own.

But two things kept me moving forward: my fear of being left behind and my desire not to let my family down. My dad was a pastor, and everyone in our community knew my family. I didn't want to be the kid who embarrassed his family or brought shame to our family name. So, I kept pushing, even though I was barely hanging on.

I wish I'd been brave enough to ask for help. I wish I'd had the courage to admit that I was struggling. But when you don't feel like you're enough, it's easier to go with the flow and hope that things will get better on their own.

I took the SAT once because I knew I needed it for college. I didn't study for it—I just showed up and hoped for the best. When I got my results, I'd scored just enough to get into Charleston Southern University in Charleston, South Carolina. I joke that they must have felt sorry for me, but the truth is, it was the only school I applied to because my sister's boyfriend played basketball there. I didn't have a backup plan, but somehow, I made it.

Over time, I began to realize that failure wasn't final. But it wasn't until I became a career counselor myself that I truly understood. When I started working with students, I saw myself in them—the fear, the doubts, the belief that they weren't enough. That's when it hit me: all those times I'd failed weren't random moments of struggle. They were lessons, opportunities to grow, and chances to become stronger and wiser.

Now, I look back at every stage of my life—elementary, middle school, high school, college, and even my time in the military—and see that each one prepared me for something bigger. Each failure taught me something important about myself and my life. It helped me develop empathy, resilience, and the ability to see the potential in others, even when they couldn't see it in themselves.

EACH FAILURE TAUGHT ME SOMETHING IMPORTANT ABOUT MYSELF AND MY LIFE.

Takeaway

I hope you'll see from my story that I wasn't always confident, but I kept pushing forward regardless. I made mistakes, took shortcuts, and struggled, but I didn't let that define me. I learned that failure isn't something to be ashamed of—it's something to learn from. Every time you fail, you can ask yourself, "What can I do differently next time?"

So, don't be afraid to mess up. Don't be scared to fall short. Every great leader has a story of

EVERY GREAT LEADER HAS A STORY OF FAILURE, AND THOSE FAILURES MAKE THEIR VICTORIES EVEN SWEETER.

failure, and those failures make their victories even sweeter. It's never about how many times you fall—it's about how many times you get back up, dust yourself off, and keep moving forward. That's where winning leadership begins—in the moments when you choose to advocate for yourself and rise again. Learn from your mistakes, and remember—failure is never final! Ask yourself these questions:

- **What happened?** Identify what led to your failure.
- **Why did it happen?** Understand the reasons behind your mistakes.
- **What can I learn from this?** Reflect on the lessons you've gained.
- **How can I advocate for myself?** Know how to speak up when you need help.

Strategies for Bouncing Back from Setbacks

You've probably heard the saying, "When life gives you lemons, make lemonade." But let's be honest—making lemonade isn't always easy, especially when dealing with setbacks, failures, or disappointments. It can feel like those lemons are a bit too sour to handle! That's why you need a plan for turning those setbacks into something sweet. Over the years, I've developed a toolbox of strategies to help when hard times come. I call it the **P3E Strategy Model**— it's like my recipe for making lemonade out of life's most challenging situations.

The P3E Strategy Model Explained

1. **Problem:** Recognize the problem.
   Almost like a detective searching for clues, when something goes wrong, take a step back and analyze the situation. Ask yourself: *What exactly went wrong? What factors led to this outcome?* Instead of dwelling on the mistake or beating yourself up, treat it like a puzzle that needs to be solved. This mindset shift will help you learn from the experience and turn it into a learning opportunity. For example, if you failed a test, think about why. Did you need to study more? Did you miss a key concept? Use your power of observation to pinpoint the problem.

2. **Process:** Create a plan to move forward.
   Once you've identified the problem, it's time to figure out your next steps. Break down the problem into smaller, manageable pieces, and ask yourself: *What could I do differently next time? What resources do I need to solve this problem?* Maybe it's asking for help, setting up a study schedule, or practicing a new skill. Failure is just part of the process—it doesn't define you. It's how you respond that matters. Map out a strategy to create a plan that moves you forward.

3. **Product:** Define your success.
   How will you know when you've bounced back from this setback? Setting a clear goal is essential to know you've overcome the challenge. For example, if you struggled with a project, your "product" might be

completing the next project with more confidence or getting a better grade. Use your ability to analyze what worked and what didn't to create a clear picture of what success looks like. Ask yourself: *What does "winning" look like for me in this situation?* Don't be afraid to celebrate even the small wins—every step forward is progress!

4. **Execution:** Establish guidelines to maintain your progress.

This is where you set up a game plan to avoid repeating the same mistakes. What rules or habits do you need to put in place to keep moving forward? Notice patterns and create a set of personal standards. Maybe it's setting aside time daily to study, asking for feedback more often, or being more organized with your tasks. Also, seek out someone you trust—a friend, teacher, coach, or mentor—to help you stay accountable. Ask them to check in and give you honest feedback on your progress. This outside perspective can be a game-changer in keeping you on track.

Example of the P3E Strategy Model in Action

Let's say you didn't make the cut for the basketball team. Here's how you can use the P3E Strategy Model:
- **Problem:** You didn't make the team. Why? Maybe you didn't practice enough or weren't strong in specific skills like shooting or defense. Analyze what particular areas you need to improve.

- **Process:** Create a plan. For example, you could practice an extra thirty minutes daily, focus on your shooting technique, or ask a friend to help you run drills.
- **Product:** Define your success. Maybe it's making the team next year or improving your shooting percentage in pick up games with friends.
- **Execution:** Set up guidelines to help you reach your goal. You might commit to practicing three times a week, watching tutorials to improve your skills, or finding a coach to give you pointers.

By using the P3E Strategy Model, you're not just dealing with failure—you're learning from it and growing stronger with a plan. Turn setbacks into opportunities, and with this model, you'll be able to bounce back from anything life throws your way if you put it into practice.

||||||||||||||||||||||||||||||||||||||||||||||||||||||||||||||||||||||||||||||||

Coaching Tip: Challenge yourself to look for things others miss and turn your setbacks into your greatest comebacks. Think of a problem in your life that might be helped by the P3E Strategy. Work with a friend to map out a solution. So, when life gives you lemons, grab your P3E Strategy Model and start making that lemonade. You've got this!

||||||||||||||||||||||||||||||||||||||||||||||||||||||||||||||||||||||||||||||||

Learning to Lose at Ultimate Frisbee

Let me share a story about a group of students from Wil Lou Gray Opportunity School in West Columbia, South Carolina I coached at our Empowered To Win Teen Nights at the Boys and Girls Clubs of the Midlands. We were playing a game called "Pass Along," and there were two teams. One team was winning every time, and the other kept losing. When it was time to play Ultimate Frisbee, there was a student named Karen on the losing team who asked if she could be the leader. I hesitated, but her enthusiasm convinced me to give her a chance.

As soon as Karen began leading, I noticed she kept encouraging her team, even when they continued to lose. Little by little, Karen's positive attitude spread, and they began to score. Eventually, they won the game—not because they were the most skilled but because they didn't give up. Karen's determination and willingness to keep trying, even after losing, inspired her team to do the same.

Losing isn't about giving up but learning, adjusting, and trying again. That's what makes a winning leader.

What Makes a Great Leader

When you think about leadership, you might picture a coach, a famous influencer, or even your school principal. But have you ever wondered how people have thought about leadership throughout history? Believe it or not, ideas about what makes a great leader have changed significantly over time. Let's look at how people have thought about leadership and how those ideas have evolved.

1. **The Born Leader Model (1800–1940): "Leaders Are Born, Not Made"**
Imagine living when people believed that only specific individuals were born to be leaders. They thought that if you weren't born with particular traits, you'd never be able to lead. People believed leaders were special, almost like they had some "leader DNA" that made them naturally better at leading than everyone else.

To prove this idea, researchers studied famous leaders, including executives, politicians, and religious leaders, expecting to find that they all had the same characteristics. But guess what? They couldn't find clear evidence that leaders were born that way. It turns out that being born into a particular family or having specific traits doesn't automatically make you a great leader.

2. **The Behavior Model (1940-1970): "Leaders Are Made, Not Born"**
After the beginning of World War II, people started to think differently about leadership. Researchers believed that it wasn't just about having the right traits—it was about the behaviors and actions of leaders. They started studying what leaders *did* and how they behaved, hoping to find out what made them effective.

A researcher named Kurt Lewin identified three main leadership behaviors:
- **The Autocratic Style:** This leader makes decisions alone and tells others what to do. It's like a coach who always calls the plays and expects everyone to follow.

- **The Democratic Style:** This leader involves others in decision-making. It's like being on a team where everyone's opinion matters and the leader helps guide the group to a decision.
- **The Laissez-Faire Style:** This leader lets others take charge and doesn't provide much direction. It's like a teacher who gives you a project and says, "Figure it out on your own."

But here's the thing: Even though these styles were identified, researchers couldn't agree on the "best." Sometimes, autocracy worked, and other times, democracy was more effective. It all depended on the situation. Therefore, the researchers could not articulate the best way to lead effectively.

3. **The Contingency Model (1960-Present): "It Depends on the Situation"**
By the 1960s, people realized there was no single "right" way to lead. This is where the **contingency model** comes in. It suggests that the best way to lead depends on your situation, the people you're leading, and your personal style.

For example, leading a group of friends during a fun weekend activity might require a different approach than leading a class project with strict deadlines. The contingency model suggests that influential leaders adapt their style to fit the situation.

What Does This Mean for You?

The history of leadership shows us one important thing: there's no single way to be a great leader. Researchers discovered that great leaders often share traits like intelligence, dependability, and humor. However, they also learned that different situations require leaders to use these traits differently. Whether you're someone who's naturally good at taking charge or you're more comfortable observing and supporting others, you have the potential to be an effective leader. The key is to be flexible, adaptable, and willing to learn from different experiences.

Today, most people believe that leadership combines all three models. While you might be born with certain qualities, the behaviors you develop and the situations you encounter will shape the kind of leader you become. This means that no matter where you start, you have the power to grow into the leader you were meant to be. Whatever path you choose, remember there is no one-size-fits-all approach to leadership.

Remember: your failures do not define you. You're defined by how you respond to them. The most successful leaders aren't the ones who never fail; they're the ones who learn how to lose, adjust, and come back stronger. So, embrace your skills, learn from your mistakes, and use every loss as a stepping stone to victory. You are empowered to be a winning leader, so let's go!

|||||||||||||||||||||||||||||||||||||||||||||||||||||||||||||||||||||||||||||||||||||||||||||

**Coaching Tip: Challenge yourself
to think about the leaders you
admire— your teachers, coaches,
family members, or friends. Which
of these leadership styles do they
show? How do they adapt their
style depending on the situation?
Understanding these different
approaches will help you become a
more effective leader in your own life.**

|||||||||||||||||||||||||||||||||||||||||||||||||||||||||||||||||||||||||||||||||||||||||||||

Winning Leadership in Action

1. Share your "Lemonade" Story on social media, in a group chat, or with friends about a time when you turned a challenging situation into something positive. Use the hashtag #LemonadeMoment and encourage your friends to do the same. You'll inspire others to see the bright side of setbacks and build a community that supports each other through tough times.

2. Take the Observer Challenge by watching a movie, TV show, or a sports game and identifying moments when the characters or players faced setbacks. How did they handle it? What did they learn? It's fun to see how others handle failure.

Plus, you'll realize that even your favorite heroes mess up sometimes!

3. Create a "Bounce-Back Plan" Using the P3E Strategy Model. Thinking about a recent challenge you faced, use the P3E Strategy Model (Problem, Process, Product, Execution) to create a bounce-back plan. Write out each step and set a small goal to help you progress. This will help you develop fundamental strategies for handling setbacks, making you more resilient whenever you face a challenge.

4. Make a vision board filled with quotes, pictures, and personal reminders that inspire you to keep going when you face challenging times. Hang it somewhere you can see it every day. It will remind you that you have the strength to overcome challenges and motivate you to keep pushing forward, no matter what.

THE OBSERVER LEADERSHIP STYLE

Superpower of the Observer Leader: Perceptive Insight

Pros and Cons of the Observer Leadership Style

Pros of Being an Observer	Examples in Action	Cons of Being an Observer
Highly perceptive and detail-oriented.	Observers notice body language in group discussions, picking up on who feels unheard or uncomfortable and adjusting the conversation to include everyone.	May over analyze situations, leading to delayed decisions.
Skilled at listening and understanding.	During a team meeting, an observer listens to everyone's ideas, summarizing the key points to ensure clarity and focus.	Can struggle to assert their own ideas or take initiative.

Pros of Being an Observer	Examples in Action	Cons of Being an Observer
Creates a balanced and thoughtful environment.	Observers in a school club encourage quieter members to contribute, fostering a more inclusive and balanced dynamic.	Risk being seen as passive or uninvolved in leadership roles.
Able to identify potential problems early.	Observers recognize when group members are frustrated or confused and suggest a break or a reset to regain focus and morale.	Can become overly cautious, avoiding necessary risks.
Promotes collaboration by valuing all voices.	An observer organizes a brainstorming session and ensures that everyone, not just the loudest voices, contributes their ideas.	May hesitate to make quick decisions in high-pressure situations.

Tips for Thriving as an Observer Leader

1. Practice balancing observation with action, and don't hesitate to take decisive steps.
2. Speak up confidently since your unique insights are valuable to your team.

3. Build trust by using your natural listening skills to show others you care about their perspectives and ideas.
4. Create SMART goals for yourself that push you to lead actively.
5. Trust your instincts, and don't over analyze the situation.
6. Collaborate with action-oriented teammates to complement your thoughtful leadership style.

Looking back on this step, what do you consider your most valuable takeaway? Write your answer below:

_____

_____

_____

_____

_____

_____

_____

_____

_____

_____

_____

_____

_____

Build Your Personal Brand

Your brand is the result of your reputation!

EVERYONE HAS A personal brand—yes, even you! Your brand is not a logo, and it goes far beyond your appearance or social media profile. It's about your reputation, values, and impact on the world around you. Your brand is your identity—who you are, what you stand for, and how others perceive you. Think of your brand as a tagline or slogan for your life. What do you want people to think of when they hear your name?

Building a brand is like building your platform. Maybe you've experienced something challenging, like bullying, and you want to share your story to help others find the confidence to overcome it. Perhaps you're passionate about addressing social issues like poverty, hunger, or environmental conservation. Maybe you're committed to fighting for animal rights or raising awareness about domestic violence. Whatever drives you, your brand is built on what's most important to you. It's about standing up for your convictions and letting the world know who you are.

What Is Your Brand?

Almost every famous person has a robust brand. Take Stephen Curry, for example. He's known as basketball's most excellent shooter, and they call him "Chef Curry" because he "cooks" his opponents on the court. His signature icon includes his initials, a net, and a sweet smile, symbolizing his love for the game. Curry's brand is all about passion, hard work, and excellence.

Or think about Elon Musk—he's built his brand around advancing technology and innovation. Whether you agree with him or not, you know that he stands for pushing boundaries and transforming industries.

My brand, as Coach Kelly, is all about empowerment. I'm known for empowering students and building leaders to push beyond their limits. I've had students and adults tell me that when they felt like giving up, something I said inspired them to keep going. That's my brand: empowering and serving people to be the best version of themselves and to become stronger leaders.

What do all these people have in common? They built their brands by staying true to themselves and their values, working hard, and surrounding themselves with supportive teams. Since your image will follow you, think about what your brand says about you.

Whether you want to become a welder, a banker, or a politician, you need to start thinking about what you want the world to see about you. Your brand is constantly evolving and will adapt as you grow, learn, and gain new experiences. Remember, your brand will only be as strong as the effort you put into protecting it. Safeguard your brand and keep it consistent with your values and goals.

Why Building Your Brand Matters

Your brand follows you wherever you go. As you build your brand, consider the person you want to become and start with the end in mind. Where do you want your brand to take you? Whether you want to enter the military, attend college, or go to trade school, your brand will shape how people perceive you and the opportunities that will come your way.

If you've already made mistakes or don't necessarily see yourself as a leader, it's not too late to start rebuilding your brand. Everyone has the power to change and grow, and your brand is constantly evolving. You will find that your brand will naturally adapt as you gain new experiences and learn more about yourself.

||||||||||||||||||||||||||||||||||||||||||||||||||||||||||||||||||||||||||||||||||

Coaching Tip: Challenge yourself to determine your brand or platform. Consider what you are passionate about. What brings you joy? As you

build this brand and think about the positive person you want to become, start with the end in mind. Find a teacher, friend, or mentor who will hold you accountable for your actions and keep you focused on your goals.

||||||||||||||||||||||||||||||||||||||||||||||||||||||||||||||||||||||||||||||||||

How Do You Build Your Brand?

Building your brand requires honesty and self-awareness. Consider the reputation you want to build. What do people notice and say about you when you're not in the room? Be honest with yourself. It's hard to hide who you are; people can sense when you're not genuine.

Ask yourself, what impact do I want to make? Your brand should inspire others to become better, stronger, and more motivated to achieve their goals. For example, I knew a young woman who struggled with low self-esteem because of her appearance. She believed she had an ugly smile and eventually got braces. She built her platform around helping others with confidence issues, which led her to study orthodontics. She turned her challenge into her brand, helping others to feel good and confident about themselves.

Self-Discipline Is Key

When you're working toward building your brand, it can be challenging. Sometimes, you'll have to make sacrifices. Maybe you want to be a Division I football player, but that means spending extra hours in the gym while your friends hang out. Perhaps you're on the debate team and must put in extra time to prepare your arguments while others relax. Self-discipline is the key to success. It's about doing the hard things consistently, even when inconvenient.

Your brand is your identity, and it will inspire, motivate, and give purpose to the people around you. Whether leading in your community, school, or online, your brand tells the world what you stand for and why you matter. Protect, grow, and let it be a force for good.

Coach Kelly's BRAND Acronym

To help you build your brand, I've developed a simple acronym—BRAND. Your brand is built by how you act, communicate, and present yourself. Let's break it down:

B—Be Professional, Be Positive, and Be Consistent
R—Represent Your Interests, Values, Skills, and Goals
A—Authenticate Your Message and Value Proposition
N—Network To Amplify Your Reach
D—Dedicate Your Time To Learn and Grow

Now, let's look at each step a little closer and talk more about them.

B—Be Professional, Be Positive, and Be Consistent

The B in BRAND stands for **Be Professional, Positive, and Consistent**—three critical ingredients for success in anything you pursue. Whether you want to be an electrician, an actor, a painter, or a nurse, you must adopt the mindset of a professional. And that starts now—not later.

How you present yourself matters—both in person and online. Whether at school, at home, or on social media, always strive to act professionally and maintain a positive attitude. You never know who's watching, and first impressions can last a long time. Being consistent means not just acting one way when things are going well and another when things are tough. It's about showing up the same way in all situations and sticking to your values.

||||||||||||||||||||||||||||||||||||||||||||||||||||||||||||||||||||||||||||||||||

**Coaching Tip: Challenge yourself
to dress the part and speak like
you mean what you say. Even
simple changes—such as showing
up on time, doing your best on
assignments, and taking pride in your
work—can transform how people
see you and how you see yourself.**

||||||||||||||||||||||||||||||||||||||||||||||||||||||||||||||||||||||||||||||||||

Be mindful of how you portray yourself online and offline. You don't want to jeopardize your future because of something as simple as a careless photo or a negative comment. It only takes one mistake to hurt your brand. Conversely, a positive and authentic online presence can open doors to scholarships, jobs, and leadership opportunities. So stand up for what is right and stay true to your values. Don't let short-term distractions or inconsistencies tarnish the image you want to project. Every choice you make reflects your character, so act accordingly.

Who you hang out with also matters. You've probably heard the saying, "You are the average of the five people you spend the most time with." If the people around you are positive, focused, and driven, that energy rubs off on you. But it's also easy to take on those same attitudes if they're negative, unmotivated, or uninterested in school or personal growth.

Look at your circle of friends. Are they lifting you or holding you back? Do they encourage you to be your best or distract you from your goals?

R—Represent Your Interests, Values, Skills, and Goals

Your brand directly reflects who you are and what you stand for. The R in BRAND means **"Representing your interests, values, skills, and goals."** Every action you take, post you share, and conversation you have should align with these elements of your identity. A strong brand is built on authenticity—being true to yourself and letting others see the real you.

Take your interests seriously and ensure that your actions align with them. Don't just say you care about something—actively work to protect it. For example, suppose you care about fairness and helping others. In that case, your actions should always show that, whether standing up for someone mistreated or volunteering to improve your community.

If you're passionate about environmental conservation, you might volunteer at local cleanups, share sustainability tips online, or join an ecology club. Each of these actions highlights what you care about, showing others what truly matters to you. By aligning your everyday habits and interactions with your core values, you're letting your passions guide you and naturally shaping a brand that reflects who you are.

Consistently living your values is crucial for building a brand people can trust. Integrity, respect, and empathy are values that great leaders hold tightly. Whether online, in school, or with friends, ensure your actions represent these values. People follow leaders who live their values, not just talk about them.

Skills are the practical side of your brand. They are the things you're good at—the talents and abilities that set you apart. What are your strengths? Maybe you're a great communicator, problem-solver, or organizer. Or perhaps you're skilled in math, art, or coding. Your skills are why people hire you or recognize you in your community.

When you examine your skills, consider how they align with your interests and values. For example, suppose you value helping others and are skilled in technology. In that case, you might volunteer to teach tech classes at a community center or help friends and family troubleshoot their devices. Aligning your skills with your values and interests is a powerful way to create a robust and authentic brand.

Your goals are the compass that guides your brand. What do you want to achieve? Where do you see yourself in five or ten years? Whether your goal is to go to college, start your own business, or enter the workforce, knowing your direction is critical to building a solid brand.

|||||||||||||||||||||||||||||||||||||||||||||||||||||||||||||||||||||||||||||||||||||||||||||||

Coaching Tip: Challenge yourself to job shadow someone in a field that interests you. The idea is to align your current actions with your future goals, making sure that everything you do today supports your goals for tomorrow.

|||||||||||||||||||||||||||||||||||||||||||||||||||||||||||||||||||||||||||||||||||||||||||||||

A— Authenticate Your Message and Value Proposition

The next letter in BRAND is A. In Coach Kelly's acronym, A stands for **"Authenticate Your Message and Value Proposition."** This step is all about being true to yourself—authenticity is the foundation of trust. If you're trying to be someone you're not, people will pick up on that quickly, and it can damage your brand. But when you stay true to yourself and let your genuine self shine through, you'll earn respect and credibility.

People are drawn to those who are real—who show both their strengths and their struggles. Strive for a deep sense of responsibility for what's right and true. Stand by your values and understand the importance of staying true to yourself. Don't pretend to be something you're not. Remember, authenticity builds trust.

I recently spoke with a student who had prepared her message and value proposition, but something was missing—it didn't feel real. Her words were polished but lacked the genuine spark of truly believing her words. She was trying to sound "right," but she lost what made her unique. Being authentic doesn't mean being perfect, but it does mean being real.

Understanding what makes you stand out is critical to building an authentic brand. Ask yourself, "What makes me different from others?" Think about your unique strengths and qualities. These will set you apart in any situation.

Your value proposition answers: Why should others care about what you bring? Whether applying for a job, submitting a college application, or starting your own business, people want to know why you're a good fit. But first, you need to know it yourself. What value will you get from going to college or entering the military? How does what you offer align with what that organization or opportunity needs?

Let's say you're applying to a college. Your value proposition could be how your unique strengths (empathy, resilience, and leadership) will contribute to the campus community. If you're entering the military, your message might be about your commitment to discipline, teamwork, and service. Your message—who you are and what you believe in—will help others understand why you're a valuable addition to their organization or community.

The key is to connect your message to what matters to you. You don't just want to go to college or the military because it sounds good—you have a purpose. Maybe it's about breaking generational barriers, helping others, or learning the skills you need to impact the world. That's your value. Communicate that clearly, and you'll stand out.

N—Network To Amplify Your Reach

The N in BRAND stands for **"Network to amplify your reach."** No one succeeds alone. Some of the most successful leaders credit much of their growth to the networks they've built over time—the people they've connected with, learned from, and leaned on. A strong network can help you in ways you may not even realize. Whether it's mentors, friends, teachers, professors, coaches, or social media influencers, your network is a powerful tool that can open doors, offer guidance, and amplify your brand.

Think of your network as the people who believe in you and your goals—those who can help you grow and provide opportunities for you to expand your reach. When others see the value in your work, they are more likely to recommend you, support your goals, and offer connections that might not have been available otherwise.

Look out for others and work hard to maintain solid and loyal relationships. This gives you a unique strength in networking because you know the importance of building connections based on trust and mutual support. You're not just looking for what you can get out of a relationship—you're focused on how you can help others while growing your brand.

You don't need to wait until you're older or more experienced to build your network. It's something you can begin today. You can network in a lot of ways. If you want to pursue a tech career, connect with people in the industry, attend events, follow tech leaders on social media, and learn from their experiences. The more people you connect with, the more quickly your brand grows and reaches others.

You might join interest groups, clubs, or online communities to find other like-minded people. Let others know your interests in the community or on social media. You can expand and grow when you connect with others and share your values, interests, and goals. This amplifies your reach. Identify people you admire and learn from them. Use social media to your advantage. Follow people in industries or careers you are interested in and engage with their content. Be proactive and reach out! Seek others that can help you grow. You never know who might have a connection that can help you.

D—Dedicate Your Time to Learn and Grow

The final letter in BRAND is D, which stands for **"Dedicate your time to learn and grow."** Building a brand doesn't happen overnight—it requires time, effort, and a commitment to continuous improvement. Growth is essential for developing not only your brand but also your skills, knowledge, and character. Whether studying harder in school, practicing a hobby, or picking up a new skill, you must focus on self-improvement and be open to growth.

Understand the importance of investing in yourself and those you care about. Just as you work hard to protect and support others, you must be committed to your personal development. Values like loyalty, trust, and service grow stronger when you actively dedicate yourself to learning and becoming the best version of yourself. You will become a reliable, constantly improving leader by adapting and growing.

Think about the areas where you want to grow. Are you passionate about public speaking? Take the time to watch TED Talks, practice in front of a mirror, or join a debate team. Are you interested in technology? Start researching online courses, watch YouTube tutorials, or join tech clubs. Growth happens when you intentionally seek out opportunities to learn and challenge yourself. Dedicate time each day or week to invest in your development, no matter the area you're passionate about.

Don't wait for opportunities to find you. Seek them out—volunteer to speak in class, join a public speaking club, or practice giving speeches at home. The more you invest in your growth, the more your brand will reflect your skills and dedication.

Growth requires effort. To become the best version of yourself, you must continuously grow and develop. No one becomes the GOAT (Greatest of All Time) overnight. Take Simone Biles, for example—she's the most decorated gymnast in history, but her success didn't happen by chance. She put in the work—training six hours daily, perfecting her craft. It's the same for any dream you have. You have to put in the effort to get the results.

||||||||||||||||||||||||||||||||||||||||||||||||||||||||||||||||||||||||||||||||

Coaching Tip: Challenge yourself to dive deeper into what you care about. Start small—maybe spend an hour researching your interest or listening to experts share their insights. These small actions will set you apart and give you a deeper understanding of your chosen path.

||||||||||||||||||||||||||||||||||||||||||||||||||||||||||||||||||||||||||||||||

Growth can be uncomfortable, but that discomfort is often where the most progress happens. While running track and playing sports in high school, I realized I ran my fastest when competing against better athletes. Sometimes, the best way to grow is to be surrounded by people who push you. So, don't always seek to be the most intelligent or skilled person in the room—put yourself in environments that challenge you. Being around stronger, more intelligent, or experienced people can help you push past your limits and unlock your true potential.

By dedicating time to learning and growth, you'll always be equipped to help others achieve their goals. Become a lifelong learner because staying prepared means staying one step ahead. Whether learning more about the career you want to pursue, gaining new skills, or developing your values, dedicating yourself to growth helps you be the best you can be.

Before he officially won the heavyweight championship, Mike Tyson was asked if he saw himself as a future champion. His response was simple: he became the champion before he became the champion. Let that sink in.

That's the mindset you need for your own growth. Envision your success, put in the work, and keep learning along the way. That's how you will become a champion of your brand. As you grow, your brand grows with you—and the possibilities are limitless.

Winning Leadership in Action

1. Write down three goals you want to achieve. Now, think about what small, daily actions you can take to move toward those goals. Remember, it's not about making giant leaps constantly—it's about showing up consistently. Share your goals with a friend.

2. Set a timer for five minutes. Then, write a short "elevator pitch" to describe your brand in thirty seconds or less. Focus on your values, interests, and goals. At the end of five minutes, team up with a partner and practice delivering your pitch to each other.

3. Participate in a debate. Imagine this scenario: You are a high school senior applying for scholarships and college admissions or a college senior applying for an internship. You've worked hard to build a positive reputation with your teachers,

professors, friends, and community. However, one day, you post a picture on social media that shows you at a party where underage people are drinking. You didn't participate in the drinking, but you were there. Now the photo is public. Team One will argue how to protect your brand and repair any potential damage from this post. What steps can you take to align your actions with your values and rebuild trust in your community? Team Two will argue what could happen if you don't act and ignore the situation. How might this post impact your brand, future opportunities, and how people perceive you? After both teams present, discuss how this scenario ties into the protector leadership style. How would a protector handle this situation to safeguard their brand and stay true to their values?"

4. Create a mock social media profile for yourself. Imagine where you want to be in five to ten years. Design it around the professional brand you want to build.

THE PROTECTOR LEADERSHIP STYLE

Superpower of the Protector Leader: Unwavering Loyalty and Guardianship

Pros and Cons of the Protector Leadership Style

Pros of Being a Protector	Examples in Action	Cons of Being a Protector
Deeply cares about the well-being of others.	A protector notices when a team member is overwhelmed and steps in to redistribute tasks or offer emotional support.	May take on too much responsibility, leading to burnout.
Builds trust and loyalty within a team.	By consistently advocating for fairness, a protector earns the respect and trust of their peers, creating a strong sense of community.	Can sometimes prioritize others' needs over their own goals.

Pros of Being a Protector	Examples in Action	Cons of Being a Protector
Strong sense of fairness and justice.	A protector ensures that a group project workload is distributed evenly, making sure everyone feels valued.	May become overly focused on resolving conflicts, delaying progress.
Encourages teamwork and collaboration.	During a school fundraiser, a protector motivates the group by emphasizing the importance of supporting the community and working together.	Can hesitate to make tough decisions that might upset others.
Promotes a safe and supportive environment.	A protector creates a "no-judgment zone" during brainstorming sessions, allowing even shy team members to share their ideas freely.	Might avoid confrontation, even when it's necessary.

Tips for Thriving as a Protector Leader

1. Set boundaries to balance supporting others and caring for your responsibilities and well-being.

2. Practice delegation by trusting your team to handle tasks independently.
3. Focus on the big picture by remembering the team's goals and deadlines.
4. Speak up confidently and make tough decisions when it's in the group's best interest.
5. Celebrate wins by acknowledging individual and team achievements to build morale and camaraderie.
6. Embrace constructive conflict by understanding that not all disagreements are harmful.

Looking back on this step, what do you consider your most valuable takeaway? Write your answer below:

_____

_____

_____

_____

_____

_____

_____

_____

_____

_____

_____

_____

STEP
4

Create a Thriving
Community

*The people you invite on the journey will
determine if you reach the destination!*

A LEADER IS NEVER alone on their journey. As
you grow, you'll realize that winning leadership isn't
just about your skills—it's about the people around
you who help you succeed. Leaders build communities that
empower, challenge, and support one another. But what
does it mean to create a thriving community?

Building a community is more than just being part of
a group. It's about belonging—finding your place among
people who share your values, interests, and goals. Think
about your friends, school clubs, campus organizations,

or sports teams. Do they push you to be better? Do they support your ambitions? If so, that's a community!

The people around you influence your journey. That's why it's so important to have people around you who encourage you to be the best version of yourself. In return, you should help them reach their goals too.

> HAVE PEOPLE AROUND YOU WHO ENCOURAGE YOU TO BE THE BEST VERSION OF YOURSELF. IN RETURN, YOU SHOULD HELP THEM REACH THEIR GOALS TOO.

Winning leaders understand that a strong community can help everyone achieve their goals. They invite people along on the journey—not by forcing them to follow, but by creating an environment where everyone feels included and valued. They make a community by fostering collaboration and bringing people together for a common purpose. They know that people are stronger together than they are apart.

The Importance of Diversity in Your Community

Imagine if everyone was exactly like you. It would not be very interesting if we were all alike. Who would do the things that you aren't good at? When you build a community with people from different backgrounds, cultures, ages, and perspectives, you open yourself up to new ideas and ways of thinking. This diversity makes you more creative, empathetic, and a better leader.

Diversity isn't just about race or gender—it's about having people around you who think differently, challenge you, and help you grow. Maybe you're passionate about sports, but your best friend loves history. Through that connection, you get to see the world from another angle and gain insights you never would have otherwise. A diverse community exposes you to new ideas, brings growth, and makes you a better leader. In short, it helps you understand why people do the things they do.

When I joined the military, I met people with many perspectives that differed significantly from mine. Getting to know them wasn't always easy, but it challenged me to grow in ways I never thought possible. I discovered that some things I was comfortable with were unfamiliar or challenging for them—and the same was true in reverse. From this, I learned a valuable lesson: just because someone's perspective differs from mine doesn't mean it is wrong. Being around people with different viewpoints made me more respectful, open-minded, and understanding. It helped me understand and value that not all people are the same. It is these differences that make a community stronger.

JUST BECAUSE SOMEONE'S PERSPECTIVE DIFFERS FROM MINE DOESN'T MEAN IT IS WRONG.

I remember leading a group in a service project. I was sure we should do it a certain way, but one of the group members had a different perspective. He suggested asking the team what they needed instead of assuming we knew what they needed. He was right. The project ended much better than if we had done it my way. It was all because we had a diverse group, and I listened to the perspectives of my team members rather than thinking I knew everything. That made all the difference.

Another time, I volunteered at a food bank with a young lady who was very excited to participate and help. However, the work she was asked to do ended up being too much, and she had an anxiety attack. That instance forced me to be mindful of others' strengths and limitations. Just because I have a great idea doesn't mean it is best for everyone.

Becoming a winning leader means understanding people's motivations, fears, goals, limitations, and challenges. The more you expose yourself to diverse perspectives, the better equipped you'll be to lead different kinds of people.

The Role of Trust in Building a Strong Community

You can't build a strong community without trust. If people in your community can't rely on you, your leadership will fall apart. Trust isn't something that happens overnight. It is built through consistency, honesty, and reliability.

Think about your closest friends. Why do you trust them? It is probably because they show up for you, listen, and keep their word. That's the kind of trust you need to build a strong, thriving community. You must be reliable and follow through on what you say.

When you trust someone, you depend on them to make decisions and do things that will keep you physically and mentally safe. Knowing that the people in your community will protect your interests and values gives you peace. When trust is lost, it also affects communication. When you have a dialogue with people you can trust, empowerment and growth occur. Broken trust makes it difficult to meet people's needs.

One crucial way to build trust is to listen to people so you can better understand their points of view. Growth happens when group members care about each other's interests and prioritize the interests of others. It can happen only when group members feel that others care and are concerned about them. Everyone needs to be heard and believe their ideas matter and are being considered. We all want to feel welcomed and appreciated.

Strong communities require a lot of give-and-take. It's not just about what others can do for you but also about what you can do for others. Mutual support and trust strengthen bonds and help communities thrive.

Online Communities versus In-Person Communities

Do you spend a great deal of time on your cell phone or laptop communicating with an online community? I used to think online friendships were less meaningful than in-person contacts. However, in recent years, my perspective has changed. Our youngest son didn't get his driver's license right away. This fact bothered me because it was so different from my own experience. Growing up, I wanted to get my license as soon as possible so I could go out with friends. However, being face-to-face wasn't our son's priority since his friends were already together online playing video games. This experience helped me redefine my definition of community.

A community can be as simple as finding other people who enjoy playing video games. From a global perspective, an online or social media group can help connect with people worldwide. Remember, having a healthy balance of in-person vs. online friendships is essential to make you more well-rounded. Communities thrive on mutual support. It's not just about what others can do for you—it's about what you can do for others. Think of it as a cycle: the more support you give, the more you'll receive. It's a win-win.

So, how do you balance the benefits of social media with the need for in-person interaction? While online platforms make it easy to connect with people worldwide, in-person interactions allow for deeper connections through body language, tone, and shared experiences. Many successful students find that a balance of online and in-person friendships offers the best of both worlds.

For example, if you're part of a gaming community, that's great! But why not set up an in-person event or gathering with your online friends? If you're passionate about an issue like climate change, join a local group or organize a volunteer event to bring your online cause into the real world. Use social media to connect but strengthen connections by meeting real-life people when possible.

Online communities are fantastic for connecting with people who share your interests—gaming, art, music, or activism. But don't forget about the power of face-to-face relationships. Body language, tone, and shared experiences create a deeper bond that digital platforms can't always match.

How do you connect yourself with a particular community? Let's say you're struggling with a subject in school, and someone in your community offers to help. In return, maybe you help them with something they're working on, like studying for a test or solving a problem. This give-and-take creates stronger bonds and a sense of shared responsibility.

Socializing in person doesn't mean you can't benefit from social media or networking platforms—they're valuable tools for building a supportive network. A robust support system can be essential to reaching your goals, and one of your best resources is your school guidance counselor, teacher, professor or academic advisor. They offer free, expert advice and bring valuable wisdom and experience. Make it a priority to connect with yours; they can be an incredible ally on your journey.

||||||||||||||||||||||||||||||||||||||||||||||||||||||||||||||||||||||||||||||||||||||

Coaching Tip: Challenge yourself as a leader to focus on building genuine relationships. When you lead, make sure everyone gets a turn to speak, celebrate each person's success, and invite the group to offer solutions or support for the challenges. This simple practice builds trust, fosters collaboration,

and keeps everyone actively engaged in each other's progress.

IIIIIIIIIIIIIIIIIIIIIIIIIIIIIIIIIIIIIIIIIIIIIIIIIIIIIIIIIIIIIIIIIIIIIIIIIIIIIIIIIIIIIII

Managing Conflict in a Community

Let's face it—disagreements are part of any community. But what makes a strong leader is how you deal with those conflicts. Can you listen to both sides? Can you help people find common ground?

Imagine your group of friends arguing about which movie to watch. It's a minor disagreement, but it can still cause tension. As a leader, you say, "Let's compromise—how about we watch one person's pick this time and another person's pick next time?" Conflict resolved!

It is essential to understand that we can agree to disagree. Winning leaders learn to actively listen to different viewpoints and allow others to share their thoughts and ideas without fear of criticism. They understand that you don't always have to agree; we can disagree respectfully.

In addition, winning leaders understand that they don't have to be the ones with all the great ideas. They give others space to voice their opinions. It is essential to realize that one person is not right in every situation. You must learn how to apologize and move forward. If someone has been offended, be willing to say you are sorry and recognize that you were wrong. Afterward, it is essential to return to that person and make amends. Show that you value their thoughts and ideas. Assure them you can coexist even though you may not always see eye to eye.

In a football huddle, everyone has their idea of what the next play should be, with teammates calling out different strategies and opinions flying back and forth. There can be a lot of debate about the best way forward. But when it's time for the game to resume, the team has to come together and commit to a single plan for the good of everyone. Sometimes, not everyone is happy with the chosen play, tensions rise, and tempers flare. That's when a foundation of trust and mutual respect makes all the difference. You may need to apologize or say, "Hey, you made the call, and I didn't agree, but that was the best decision." Then, you shake it off and get back to the game. Anytime you are part of a community, disagreements are inevitable. There will be times when others don't see things your way, and that's okay.

I remember when my coach gave me specific instructions on approaching a task, but I decided to do it my way instead. When it didn't work out, I had to admit, "You know what? You were right, and I was wrong." Moments like these taught me that being able to apologize is where real growth begins.

So, how can you bring people together when there's conflict? Often, people in disagreement don't want to be in the same room, but change can happen if they're willing to sit down and talk it through with a neutral party. The facilitator listens to both sides and helps find a fair solution to heal the relationship. Of course, not all conflicts can be quickly resolved, but open dialogue and respect can still strengthen the group.

BEING ABLE TO APOLOGIZE IS WHERE REAL GROWTH BEGINS.

Being a leader isn't always easy. I remember one home-coming weekend in college when I faced a real test of leadership. At the time, I was president of an organization on campus. As I was studying in my room, some group members came to me visibly upset. They shared that a campus fraternity had done something profoundly disre-spectful and offensive toward our members. They looked to me, as president, to act and address the issue.

So, even though I had never handled anything like it before, I brought the issue to the student council and college administration. By doing that, we were able to hold the fraternity accountable and discuss the repercussions and how to prevent similar situations. Navigating this conflict respectfully wasn't easy. But in standing up for our members, we created positive change. Ultimately, this experience impacted our organization and strengthened our campus community, making a lasting difference for others.

Leading a Community Project

Winning leaders don't wait for change; they create it. There are countless ways students can make an impact in their community. Maybe your school could benefit from a coat drive or a campus cleanup day. These initiatives help others and provide an excellent opportunity to show leadership and rally your peers to get involved.

I've seen students organize drives for "Toys for Tots" or fill an "Angel Tree" with gifts for needy families. One group hosted a party where admission required a donation of canned goods for the food bank, and others have led coat drives for people experiencing homelessness or held car washes and bake sales to fund community projects. Even organizing a 5K or walkathon can be a fun way to raise money and awareness for important causes.

One student I knew was a quiet young man who transferred to the charter school where I was a career counselor. Despite his reserved nature, he wanted to make an impact on younger students at his new school. He came to me with the idea of creating a mentoring program. After I offered support and guidance, he took the lead. He recruited other high school guys who shared his interest, held an initial meeting with ten to fifteen students, and together, they developed a mentorship group. They visited elementary and middle schools twice a month to read with students, lead team-building activities, and teach character development. The project was a huge success: younger students felt supported and encouraged, and the older students grew as leaders. That young man went on to serve in the military, study business, and eventually continue mentoring young people in building their dreams. All of it started with a simple idea and the courage to make it happen.

Whether it's organizing a study session or a fundraiser, the size of the project doesn't matter as much as the initiative behind it. What counts is the willingness to step up and make a positive impact.

Finding a Mentor

Think about someone to whom you look up to. Maybe it's your teacher, career counselor, coach, or someone you respect in your community. Find individuals doing something you want to do and ask them to mentor you. Mentors help guide you by sharing their experiences and wisdom.

But here's the cool part—you can be a mentor, too. Winning leaders aren't just the ones in charge—they're the ones who lift others. Who could you mentor in your community? It could be a younger student, a sibling, or even a friend who needs help. Think about how you can pay it forward by mentoring someone else.

THINK ABOUT HOW YOU CAN PAY IT FORWARD BY MENTORING SOMEONE ELSE.

Dr. Carl Wells was my mentor in college, and I respect him to this day. He worked in student support services at my college. Dr. Wells always made time for me and helped me to see the authentic gifts and talents within myself. He helped me to push beyond my comfort zone and challenges. He told me to be willing to do the hard things to become great and to always believe in myself.

The best people and communities push you to do better. When everyone understands the mission of the group and values other people—that's when great things happen. You can make a difference no matter how old or young you are. It doesn't matter how smart you are; you can grow together and serve. Everyone must intentionally make others feel welcome and find what makes others tick. Most people want to be part of something bigger than themselves. That's key.

As a winning leader, you find needs and then address them. Are there older adults in the community who can no longer cut their grass? How can you help or support them? Needs always present themselves. Leaders must be willing to take the initial step. Once that step is taken, the action spreads. You'll see one turn into two.

One time, I was watching a YouTube video of a man at a park dancing by himself to some music. People stared at him, probably thinking he looked a little odd. But he didn't care; he just kept dancing, thoroughly enjoying the moment. Then something unique happened: someone else stepped forward and started dancing along with him. Soon, more people joined, and before long, a crowd of about a hundred people was dancing together in the park. It all happened because one person dared to start. He showed how one person's actions can spark something much bigger, creating a movement that impacts people in a powerful, unforgettable way.

Create Your Thriving Community

Communities grow when everyone brings their best, shares their ideas, and supports one another. So, what can you offer your community? How can your involvement in a group benefit other people? And how can the group help you grow?

Sometimes, it takes getting comfortable with being uncomfortable to push yourself forward. Put yourself in a position to challenge yourself to grow and develop. Whether joining a new club or taking on a leadership role, each step is an opportunity to grow and transform.

Leadership is more than a title—inviting others on a journey, building connections, creating trust, and inspiring a group to work toward a shared goal. As you build your community, remember that each person brings unique value. Celebrate those differences and allow your community to push you to grow in ways you never imagined. When you take the initiative to build a thriving community, you help others and discover more about yourself.

So, surround yourself with people who encourage, challenge, and support your dreams. In turn, become someone who does the same for others. This is the true power of a thriving community, where winning leadership begins.

Winning Leadership in Action

1. Explore the diversity within your community by creating a world map that marks the locations of your classmates' ancestral or family origins. As a class, discuss the unique cultural connections represented in the room, sharing stories, traditions, or customs tied to these locations. Reflect on how this rich diversity strengthens your community, fosters understanding, and brings people together through shared and unique experiences.

2. Participate in a circle of trust by forming a circle with the group and sharing something you value in a friendship. Don't forget to tell them why you think it is so important.

3. Working in a small group, have each person write down one unique aspect of themselves and assemble them to create a diversity map. Use your map to discuss how diversity strengthens the community. Then, have a spokesperson share your conclusions with the larger group.

4. Write a thank-you note to someone in your class or at work, highlighting when that person helped you feel supported. Deliver your message to your classmate or coworker before the end of the class period or at the end of your shift.

THE CONNECTOR LEADERSHIP STYLE

Superpower of the Connector Leader: Bridge Builder

Pros and Cons of the Connector Leadership Style

Pros of Being a Connector	Examples in Action	Cons of Being a Connector
Easily builds relationships	Connectors are often the ones who get everyone talking and feeling included. By encouraging others to speak up, connectors create a space where everyone feels valued.	Overextending Relationships— Connectors may feel the need to maintain too many relationships, which can be overwhelming and dilute meaningful connections.

Pros of Being a Connector	Examples in Action	Cons of Being a Connector
Encourages collaboration	Connectors bring people together for shared goals, like organizing a school coat drive or volunteering project. For instance, the mentoring group that met to support younger students demonstrates how connectors foster collaboration and team spirit.	Potential for Conflict—By bringing different personalities together, connectors might sometimes face disagreements. However, this also gives them the chance to practice conflict resolution.
Fosters belonging and inclusion	Connectors are essential for creating a sense of belonging. They make others feel included and supported by aligning shared interests, values, and goals within the group.	Difficulty Setting Boundaries— Connectors may find it hard to say no and might take on too much, risking burnout.

Pros of Being a Connector	Examples in Action	Cons of Being a Connector
Great listeners and communicators	Connectors listen actively, understanding what people need and figuring out how they fit into the bigger picture. For example, when working at a food bank, being mindful of others' strengths and needs made the experience impactful for everyone.	Risk of Over-involvement— Connectors who engage deeply in everyone's concerns can sometimes lose focus on their own goals or get caught up in other people's issues.

Pros of Being a Connector	Examples in Action	Cons of Being a Connector
Empowers and encourages others	Connectors are great at helping people find their strengths and supporting them to grow. For example, when beautifying a garden, the Connector encourages everyone to see the impact of their work, motivating the team.	Can Feel Responsible for Group Success— Connectors might place the group's needs above their own, which can sometimes limit their ability to take on solo pursuits.

Tips for Thriving as a Connector Leader

1. Build boundaries to avoid burning out by prioritizing relationships that align with your values and goals.
2. Balance your community, making time for in-person and online connections to ensure meaningful interactions.
3. Encourage conflict resolution by being a mediator and ensuring all voices are heard, especially when conflicts arise.

Looking back on this step, what do you consider your most valuable takeaway? Write your answer below:

_____

_____

_____

_____

_____

_____

_____

_____

_____

_____

_____

_____

_____

_____

_____

_____

_____

_____

_____

_____

_____

STEP 5

Develop Your Skills

*The cheat code to success is accessible
through your skills and discipline!*

I N HIGH SCHOOL, my sights were set on becoming a football player. Career exploration wasn't something I prioritized, and I didn't spend much time with my guidance counselor figuring out what might suit me best. I also wasn't on a traditional college prep track, so I didn't receive much advice from my teachers about plans. All I knew was that I wanted to go to college and make something positive of myself—but beyond that, my path was unclear.

When I started college, I decided to pursue accounting, mainly because I thought it was closely tied to business— not because I had any genuine interest in it or knew much about what accounting entailed. Once I began my accounting classes, though, I quickly realized it wasn't for me. I didn't enjoy math much, and accounting didn't excite me. So, while I knew accounting wasn't the right path, I wondered: what would be a good fit for me?

By my second year of college, I had switched majors several times. I considered changing again to education since I'd always had a passion for helping students. However, I hesitated once I learned about lesson plans. Ultimately, I decided to stick with the business degree, thinking it would open my career options.

I finally met with an academic advisor who helped me see that business administration might better fit my interests. At the time, I was aiming for a career in corporate America, something I could pursue after my years in the armed forces. I planned to graduate, reach the rank of captain in the military, and then transition into the business world. I still didn't have a clear idea of which area of business I wanted to focus on, but I was drawn to it because I associated business careers with financial success, which seemed important at the time.

After joining the military, an injury forced me to leave earlier than planned, so I pivoted toward a business career, which was highly accessible for veterans then. I started in pharmaceutical sales and then moved on to banking. While I enjoyed aspects of each job, I quickly realized something was missing. In both the military and my business roles, I didn't feel I was making a real difference in people's lives. Although I initially focused on financial success and the perks that came with it, I found that money and status alone weren't fulfilling.

One day, while golfing with some friends, I found myself talking with the executive director of a charter high school in Columbia, South Carolina. He suggested that I consider becoming a career counselor and student success coach. He recognized how my diverse experiences had prepared me perfectly for the role. As he spoke about the meaningful impact this job could have on students' lives, something clicked for me. Soon after, I decided to leave my current job and embrace this new path.

I always encourage students to gain as much experience and develop as many skills as possible while young. Approach each opportunity with a "work to learn" mindset. Explore what you genuinely enjoy and are passionate about, then see how those interests align with different career paths. If you're passionate about helping others, you might find fulfillment in teaching, social work, or healthcare. If you love the outdoors, fields like landscaping, agriculture, or environmental science might be the right fit. Remember, there's no single path for everyone, and that's the beauty of career exploration—you have choices that align with your unique talents and interests. Embrace those possibilities and discover what makes you excited about the future!

When it comes to preparing for a career, the possibilities are vast. If college is your path, there are many types to choose from: public universities, private colleges, large schools, small schools, expensive options, and more affordable ones. However, only some careers require a college degree. Many high-demand jobs require only training through a technical school, career tech, or an apprenticeship program. And while the military is an option for some, it's not for everyone.

The key is to focus first on identifying what you want to do. Once you have an idea, you can begin mapping out the best way to gain the necessary skills and experience. Embrace the freedom to create your unique journey.

Determining your skills and figuring out what you want to do may feel overwhelming, but it starts with exploring and being open to discovering new things about yourself. Start by doing some research and taking assessments to help reveal your natural talents and areas of interest. Your school career counselor is an excellent resource for connecting you to career exploration tools and guiding you through the process. Mentors, too, are invaluable for offering advice and sharing their own experiences, so talk to people in fields you're curious about—whether that's healthcare, technology, creative arts, or even entrepreneurship.

If you're interested in being an entrepreneur, explore what that might look like by learning from people who have started their own businesses. Ask them about the skills and mindset needed to make an idea successful. Try to get an understanding of how they have used their strengths to tackle challenges and how they discovered what areas they wanted to pursue. This can provide insight into what skills you'll need to develop and what paths might align with your ambitions.

To gain hands-on experience, join school organizations, participate in internships, community networking groups or volunteer in fields you're interested in. Even a part-time job or a one-day job shadow can help you see what different careers look like day-to-day and help you understand how your skills align. Remember that every opportunity is a chance to learn something new about what you enjoy (and don't enjoy), which will help you shape your future.

When bringing your passions into your career, think about what excites and motivates you. If you love helping others, consider jobs where you can make a difference, like education, social work, or healthcare. If you're passionate about the environment, you might consider roles in sustainability, environmental science, or landscaping. By blending your passions with practical experience, you'll find a path that feels meaningful and true to who you are. So, ask yourself: how can you take what you care deeply about and apply it in a career? This approach is critical to building a future you're excited about.

My passion for education grew from seeing myself in my students. Like me, many of them were unsure of what they wanted to do with their lives. I wanted to make a difference by providing them with the tools and guidance I hadn't had—to help them make informed choices about their futures. It became deeply fulfilling to encourage and motivate students, and I found absolute joy in creating opportunities for them, whether it was through job shadowing, college tours, or offering advice. I discovered my sense of purpose in giving my students what I lacked in school. My niche was education, and I learned the value of "failing forward." Many parts of my life hadn't worked out as I'd planned—the military, accounting, or even a business degree. But all those missteps ultimately prepared me to find my calling in helping others and making an impact I'd never imagined.

Many well-known people turned their passions into successful careers. Taylor Swift, driven by her love for writing and singing, became a global phenomenon in music. Kobe Bryant pursued his love for basketball and became one of the greatest players ever. Tiger Woods transformed his passion for golf into a legacy that re-energized the sport and inspired a new generation, including his son. Steve Jobs founded Apple, Jeff Bezos launched Amazon, and four college students, Tony Xu, Andy Fang, Stanley Tang and Evan Moore founded DoorDash—all driven by their deep passions. These stories remind us that we can achieve extraordinary things by following our true interests and developing our skills.

THE FIRST STEP IN PLANNING FOR YOUR FUTURE IS TO IDENTIFY THE SKILLS YOU ALREADY HAVE.

The first step in planning for your future is to identify the skills you already have. Many of mine came from tasks I did at home. My parents taught me to work in our family garden, iron clothes, clean the house, and cook meals, which developed my attention to detail and essential life skills. I also worked part-time with my uncle in his lawn care business, where I learned how to communicate and work with customers. Playing video games helped me sharpen my problem-solving skills while taking on leadership roles in high school and college and taught me about conflict resolution. Although I didn't enjoy typing classes in school, I use those skills daily. Looking back, I can see that all these experiences helped build a foundation I continue to rely on.

Of course, skills specific to certain jobs—like coding, welding, or electrical work—usually require more specialized training. When I went to college, I focused on building on the skills I already had to prepare for my desired career. Everything I did, from chores to side jobs to school projects, taught me new skills and added to my experience. Each one prepared me for my future opportunities.

Start by identifying your strengths and skills—those things that give you an edge or come quickly to you. A strength is anything you do well that sets you apart or gives you an advantage. It might be drawing, speaking, cleaning, organizing, or inspiring people. Think about the things you can do without much effort or the skills others notice in you. Maybe you have a part-time job or volunteer role that you enjoy. These experiences are helping you develop new skills, so keep an open mind and explore different activities. You'll never know what you're good at if you don't first give it a try. What do others frequently compliment you on or rely on you for?

Figuring out your strengths can sometimes be as simple as listening to feedback. In my first job in education, I didn't see myself as a motivator, but people would say, "Kelly, you have a great way of inspiring others. When you talk, students listen and get energized." So, in my school, I would be called upon to pump up the crowd at pep rallies. Over time, I began to see motivation as a strength. Hearing it from others helped me recognize it, and eventually, I began using it more intentionally, which led me to motivational speaking.

Talk to those who know you well—teachers, career counselors, guidance counselors, mentors, and family members. They can help you identify strengths you might not see in yourself. Teachers, career counselors, career coaches and online resources are especially helpful in matching your strengths with potential careers.

Online assessments can also provide valuable insights. Here are a few to consider:

- CareerOneStop Skills Matcher by the US Department of Labor helps match your skills with career options. https://www.careeronestop.org/Toolkit/Skills/skills-matcher.aspx
- MyNextMove Interest Profiler, also by the Department of Labor, lets you explore careers based on your interests. https://www.mynextmove.org/explore/ip
- College Board Career Quiz offers personalized career suggestions in just a few minutes. https://bigfuture.collegeboard.org/career-search/career-quiz
- YourFreeCareerTest.com is another straightforward tool for assessing interests and skills. https://www.yourfreecareertest.com/

These assessments and advice from your career counselor can give you a solid starting point for exploring your career options. The more you know about your strengths, the easier it will be to make informed choices about your future!

Most students your age dream of landing a high-paying job, but earning a lot of money doesn't always lead to lasting happiness. Instead, start by exploring your passions and skills. Think about how you want to make an impact in the world. How can you contribute to something greater than yourself? Imagine what happiness and a quality life would mean to you. Would you feel fulfilled by owning a big house, or do you dream of traveling and seeing the world?

Following your passion and leveraging your skills can lead you to a genuinely satisfying life. My early work and volunteer experiences shaped me in ways I never expected. Volunteering with my church youth group, working on landscaping projects with my uncle, and helping kids at the

YMCA each summer—all these experiences helped mold me into the leader I am today. The things you choose to do now will help you uncover what you love and ultimately shape your future.

Craft a Resume

Creating a resume is your chance to showcase your skills and experiences, letting others see what you bring. Start with a simple list on your computer, but remember to provide as much detail as possible. A strong resume clearly shows what you've accomplished, highlighting your education, skills, and leadership roles.

Being active in clubs and organizations adds value to your resume, showing that you're engaged and willing to take on responsibilities. Grades matter too, as they reflect your commitment to learning and improvement.

Think of your resume as a door-opener. It doesn't guarantee the job, but it opens the door to an interview, where potential employers can learn more about your personality, skills, and ambitions. Once that opportunity is there, your resume's details help interviewers see the unique value you could bring to their organization.

You don't need fancy resume software—simple tools like Microsoft Word work perfectly. What's most important is detail. First, list each experience with crucial details that show what you accomplished and the value you added. Let's look at an example of how details make a difference:

- *Anytown High School Band*
- *Anytown High School Band (9th–12th grade)*— First-chair trumpet player; Trumpet section leader;

Attended 250 hours of rehearsal from 6:30–9:30 a.m. each school day during the 2024–25 school year.

Which entry would stand out more? Clearly, the second one shows your role and demonstrates leadership, commitment, and a strong work ethic. This type of detail grabs an interviewer's attention and sets you apart. By adding details, you're setting yourself up for success with a resume that tells your story.

Land the Interview

An interview is a two-way street. Not only does it give an organization a chance to assess you, but it also allows you to evaluate if they're the right fit for you. This mutual assessment can make all the difference in whether you'll thrive in the role. Your appearance speaks before you do. Although different roles may have different dress standards, it's generally a safe bet to dress business casual or in a suit. Do some research to find out what's appropriate for the position for which you're applying. Dressing professionally shows respect for the opportunity and separates you from other candidates.

One of my students, for example, was applying for a job at the fast-food chicken restaurant Bojangles. I advised her to wear professional attire. She went the extra mile, wearing dress pants, a jacket, and even heels. In addition, she brought along a portfolio with her resume. Not only did she get the job, but her polished presentation earned her a higher position as a cashier with better pay. It's amazing what a solid first impression can do.

Know the job description inside and out so you can understand the values and goals of the organization. Employers want to know why they should hire you, so your preparation should reflect your commitment and enthusiasm for the role.

I encourage students to bring questions to the interview because it shows you're genuinely interested. At least three or four thoughtful questions can demonstrate your engagement and help you make a memorable impression.

Save the "million-dollar question" for last: "Is there any reason I wouldn't be a good fit for this position?" This question gives you a chance to address any concerns directly. For example, if one interviewer thinks you lack experience, you can reassure them by highlighting your work ethic, quick learning abilities, and relevant skills. Addressing potential hesitations can make a difference in landing the role. Be yourself—authenticity resonates with interviewers. Confidence in your skills and potential goes a long way, even if you're not an expert. Training and growth are expected, and showing a willingness to learn is often more impressive than already knowing everything. Don't forget to highlight any leadership qualities, as the ability to motivate, manage, and communicate effectively are always assets. Reflect on your strengths from the six winning leadership styles to show how you can bring unique value to the role.

> SAVE THE "MILLION-DOLLAR QUESTION" FOR LAST: "IS THERE ANY REASON I WOULDN'T BE A GOOD FIT FOR THIS POSITION?"

Networking for Growth

Networking is a powerful tool to help you land future interviews and opportunities. While it may only sometimes lead directly to a job, networking builds connections, exposes you to new ideas, and increases your visibility in your chosen field. Networking is about collaboration, learning, and finding where you might fit best or how to help others. It's also a chance to see if the organization's values align with yours.

Building relationships within your community can fuel personal and professional growth. Verbal, nonverbal, and written communication skills are crucial for making meaningful connections. Communication is the foundation of effective networking, allowing you to express yourself clearly and understand others. Developing these skills is an investment in your future, giving you a competitive edge in interviews and life.

With a strong resume, professional presentation, and confident, authentic communication, you'll be well-prepared to land the interview and make it count.

‖‖‖

Coaching Tip: Challenge yourself to choose one skill you want to improve and create a thirty-day action plan. Dedicate at least fifteen minutes each day to focused practice—whether that's reading about the skill, watching a tutorial,

**or doing hands-on exercises.
Find a friend to share a reflection
about what you have learned
and where you can improve. This
consistent approach helps you stay
accountable and continue to grow.**

||||||||||||||||||||||||||||||||||||||||||||||||||||||||||||||||||||||||||||||||||||

Moving Into the Future

As you progress in your journey, remember that developing your skills is about more than just preparing for a job—it's about shaping a life and career you're genuinely passionate about. The path may twist and turn, but with each step, you discover more about yourself, your talents, and what makes you feel fulfilled.

I didn't know exactly what I wanted to do when I first set out. I explored different fields, changed my mind, and experienced setbacks. Each experience taught me something new and pushed me closer to where I was meant to be. I learned that working to learn, as Robert Kiyosaki wisely said, was the best approach to gaining skills, insight, and self-awareness.

As you prepare for your future, try new things, ask questions, and keep an open mind. Reflect on your strengths, passions, and values, and look for ways to turn them into meaningful opportunities. Be willing to take on challenges, adapt to change, and keep growing.

The possibilities for your career are endless. Whether in college, technical training, the military, or an apprenticeship, your path is uniquely yours to create as a winning leader. With your passions as a guide, use each experience to learn more, grow your skills, and find purpose in everything you do. Ultimately, your willingness to explore and learn will set you apart and shape your future.

Winning Leadership in Action

1. Use a computer or laptop to design a business card, or an app like Blinq to design a digital business card for free showcasing your name, professional email, potential career interest, digital work and your key skills and strengths. Make it look professional and engaging. Once complete, print multiple copies and use them to connect with classmates, teachers, or mentors, helping to build your network and leave a lasting impression. Blinq will create a QR code for you to share with others. This simple yet powerful tool is a great way to start building your network by sharing your information, brand, skills and interests with others.

2. Spend five minutes interviewing a partner to explore their career interests, strengths, skills, and passions. Ask at least three thoughtful questions to help them reflect on what they enjoy, what they're good at, and where they see themselves in the future. Afterward, switch roles, and they'll interview you about your career ideas and goals. When both interviews are complete, take a few moments to share what you discovered about interviewing techniques—such as asking open-ended questions, listening actively, and

making the other person feel comfortable. Be prepared to discuss how this experience helped you see the value of interviews in uncovering insights and making connections.

3. Use a computer or laptop to create a professional-looking resume. List your skills, interests, clubs, volunteer experience, and work experience. Describe each item, especially your accomplishments—what did you achieve or contribute to each role? For example, describe how you motivated others or organized events if you held a leadership role in a club. If you volunteered, highlight any specific tasks or projects you completed. This resume will help you reflect on your achievements and prepare for future job or internship applications.

4. Take an online skills assessment such as those listed in this chapter. When you have done that, please list some of your strengths and give examples of how you've used them in real-life situations.

THE INFLUENCER LEADERSHIP STYLE

Superpower of the Influencer Leader: Charismatic Connection

Pros and Cons of the Influencer Leadership Style

Pros of Being an Influencer	Examples in Action	Cons of Being an Influencer
Motivates Others.	Influencers, like mentors who use their personal experiences, inspire others by showing how they overcame obstacles to find purpose. Their journey motivates others to explore their own potential.	Can be perceived as being overbearing—If an influencer dominates conversations or constantly shares their perspective, it can make others feel overshadowed and less likely to contribute their own ideas.

Pros of Being an Influencer	Examples in Action	Cons of Being an Influencer
Strong Communication Skills.	Creating a well-detailed resume or portfolio shows an Influencer's ability to communicate achievements effectively, drawing interest from potential employers.	Risk of Miscommunication—If an Influencer isn't careful to ensure their message aligns with the organization or community, it can lead to confusion about goals and expectations.
Builds Positive Reputation.	Students who dress professionally and communicate clearly in interviews demonstrate how influencers make a strong, positive impression that can lead to more significant opportunities.	Pressure to Maintain High Standards—The influencer may feel pressure to "always be on" or to uphold a flawless image, which can be exhausting and might lead to burnout.

Pros of Being an Influencer	Examples in Action	Cons of Being an Influencer
Fosters a Supportive Network.	Designing a business card or networking online showcases an Influencer's strength in building connections that can open doors for future opportunities.	Requires Significant Time and Effort—Building and maintaining relationships takes consistent effort, and the Influencer might struggle to balance networking with other responsibilities.
Creates Opportunities for Growth.	By taking on various roles, such as volunteering or participating in clubs, an Influencer gains diverse skills, helping them shape their career direction while inspiring peers.	May Overlook Other Perspectives— Sometimes, an Influencer's enthusiasm for their own path can lead to overlooking other perspectives, potentially missing valuable insights from teammates.

Tips for Thriving as an Influencer Leader

1. Stay authentic because influence is more powerful when it is genuine.
2. Listen as much as you speak. Influence isn't just about talking; it's also about listening.
3. Take time to refine your message and communicate clearly so your message is aligned with your goals.

Looking back on this step, what do you consider your most valuable takeaway? Write your answer below:

_____

_____

_____

_____

_____

_____

_____

_____

_____

_____

_____

_____

_____

_____

Move Your Dream Forward

Progress happens when you decide to move forward!

NOW IS THE time to act and dream big. Imagine waking up daily with a clear sense of where you're headed and why. It's like having an extra burst of energy and excitement because you know you're working toward something meaningful. This is what having a dream is all about. A real dream isn't just a daydream or a wish—it's a powerful, motivating force that gives you direction, pushes you through challenges, and fuels your desire to reach your goals.

Think of a dream as your roadmap on a road trip. Without a map, you'd drive around aimlessly, not knowing where you're going. But with that map, you know exactly where to turn, how far you must travel, and where you'll stop. It keeps you focused, even if there are unexpected detours. A dream gives you that purpose and confidence as you move forward, helping you grow, learn, and become the best version of yourself.

I created an acronym—**D.R.E.A.M.S.**—to help you remember the steps to achieving your dreams. These six keys will keep you on track as you pursue your dreams as a winning leader.

Coach Kelly's Six Keys for Winning Leaders to Achieve Their D.R.E.A.M.S.

- **D = Desire a Pathway to Success, Set Goals, and Prioritize Them**
  Desire is the spark that lights up your dreams. What type of path are you on? Do you have a deep desire to succeed? Envision what your ideal life or career will look like. What's your desired outcome? Start with this powerful desire as the fuel that drives you. Write down and prioritize your goals to move forward. What are the things you must do to work toward achieving your dreams?

- **R = Resourcefulness**
  Resourcefulness means finding ways to get the help and information you need. Ask your guidance counselor, mentor, academic advisor, teachers, family, or friends for advice. Use resources like career assessments or online research to explore what you love to do and where it might take you.

- **E = Education**
  Education is crucial to turning dreams into reality. What knowledge or skills do you need to achieve your dreams? How can you build on what you already know? Seek out classes, training, or hands-on experiences to grow your abilities and prepare for your future.
- **A = Accountability**
  Accountability means sticking with your goals and plans. If you're unsure precisely what you want, pick a path and start working toward it. Check in with a coach, mentor, or friend to help keep you on track, and remember that every small action counts. Most importantly, hold *yourself* accountable.
- **M = Mental Toughness**
  Mental toughness is all about resilience. Stay committed to your goals and decide to follow through. Don't procrastinate. Once you commit, stay strong, even when things get challenging. That determination will keep you moving forward.
- **S = Self-Discipline**
  Self-discipline is the glue that holds your dreams together. It means staying focused, creating a plan, and following through. It's about resisting distractions and making choices that align with your goals. When you develop self-discipline, you build habits that lead to long-term success. Whether studying for a test, saving money, or showing up on time, self-discipline helps you take consistent action toward your dreams.

When I talk to students, I love seeing the shift that happens when they start thinking about their dreams. I once met a student who was passionate about music but hadn't considered college. The more he talked about his love for music, the more he realized he wanted to study it more deeply to understand and master his craft. His vision evolved, and he realized that college was part of the path to achieving his dream. Having a vision allowed him to make decisions that supported his goals and kept him motivated, even when things got tough.

Having a dream helps you see beyond daily pressures—like schoolwork, social expectations, and activities—to focus on what truly matters. It lets you decide how to spend time, which classes to take, and which clubs to join. For example, if you dream of becoming a nurse, volunteering at a hospital could help you gain experience and skills to make your vision more real and achievable.

My dream began when I decided I wanted to become an officer in the military. I joined the military during college to help fund my education, but I wanted more than just being enlisted. I set my sights on becoming a captain and enrolled in the ROTC program at Lander University. This vision pushed me to take more challenging classes and enroll in leadership training. Every step I took brought me closer to my goal and prepared me for life. I had to pivot when my career path changed unexpectedly due to an injury. Yet, those skills and experiences paved the way for new opportunities in corporate America, education, and my business.

I kept my dream front and center by writing down my goals and surrounding myself with motivational reminders. This habit made me determined to keep moving forward, even when life took an unexpected turn. Having a dream doesn't mean everything will go perfectly, but it does mean that you're always working toward something that matters.

Craft Your Dream Statement

What's your vision for the future? When you picture yourself five to ten years from now, what do you see? Think about the career you have, the lifestyle you lead, and where you're living. What steps must you take to turn that vision into reality? You've already reflected on your interests and how they align with your future goals. Now, let's take it a step further.

Ask yourself: *Where do I see myself in ten years?* Be specific. What job or career do you have? What does your family life look like? What type of business do you own? Where are you living?

||||||||||||||||||||||||||||||||||||||||||||||||||||||||||||||||||||||||||||||||||||||||||||

Coaching Tip: Write your dream as if it's already happening, using vivid, positive language. For example: "I own a thriving business repairing wrecked cars, and I'm making a difference in my community by helping people get back on the road." Post this vision somewhere you'll see it every day—on your desk, locker, or even as your phone

background. Regularly seeing your dream will keep you motivated and focused, reminding you of why you're putting in the effort.

||||||||||||||||||||||||||||||||||||||||||||||||||||||||||||||||||||||||||||||||||||||||

Take a moment to craft your dream statement below:

_____

_____

_____

_____

Create Some SMART Goals

Now it's time to create some SMART goals to set you on the path to achieving your vision. SMART goals help you turn your dreams into concrete, actionable steps. Without clear goals, even the best ideas will remain just that—ideas or dreams. A SMART goal helps guide you by providing structure and clarity.

Do you think setting a SMART goal sounds complicated? Think again. SMART is an acronym for specific, measurable, achievable, relevant, and time bound. Anyone can create a SMART goal; it's all about including the correct details to keep you focused and motivated.

Let's break it down using our welding example. Imagine your vision is to become a welder who owns a business specializing in fixing wrecked cars. A crucial first step is getting the education and training you need to realize that vision. One of your goals might be:
Apply to welding programs.
While that's a good start, it's vague. Which programs will you apply for? How will you measure your progress? How will you know when you've achieved this goal? Is it relevant to your ultimate vision? What's your timeline for completing this step?

So, to make our welding example a SMART goal, we can add more detail:

Specific: Identify which welding programs you will apply to and include details like location and program type. For example, you might apply to a local technical college or trade school.

Measurable: Set a target, like applying to three different programs. Keep a checklist to track which applications have been completed and submitted.

Achievable: Make sure applying to these programs is realistic for your current situation. For example, ensure you meet the entrance requirements for these programs, such as having a high school diploma or relevant coursework. Talk with your guidance counselor if you aren't sure. Schedule a weekly time to work on the application process, including gathering documents and writing required essays.

Relevant: Check that the goal aligns with your overall vision of becoming a welder who owns a business and repairs wrecked cars.

Time Bound: Set a clear deadline for achieving this step, such as applying to these programs within the next three months.

With these details in place, your vague goal becomes:

> *"I will apply to three specific welding programs (list them) by (insert deadline here), ensuring I meet all their requirements and submit applications before the deadline."*

This approach makes your goal clear and actionable. Now it's your turn—think about your vision and create SMART goals to guide you there.

Write down three goals to help you achieve your vision for the future. Studies show that writing down your goals increases the likelihood of achieving them. Use the template below to help you make them SMART.

Goal Number One
Specific:
Measurable:
Achievable:
Relevant:
Time Bound:

Goal Number Two
Specific:
Measurable:
Achievable:
Relevant:
Time Bound:

Goal Number Three
    Specific:
    Measurable:
    Achievable:
    Relevant:
    Time Bound:

Setting these goals means taking the first steps toward turning your vision into reality. Every goal you set and achieve will bring you closer to the future you're working toward!

Sharing Your Goals

Imagine yourself on a football team where the ultimate goal is to win the championship. Every player wants it, but you don't just wake up one day and claim the trophy. Winning takes time, dedication, conditioning, practice, and most importantly—a coach. I'm here as Coach Kelly, guiding you through this journey. As a football coach calls play, encourages players, and helps them make smart adjustments on the field, I'm here to be your coach, helping you set goals, push through obstacles, and ultimately cross the finish line.

Now, I want you to think about finding a personal coach in your life—someone who will be on your team to help you reach your goals. This could be a teacher, family member, mentor, or even a friend who's motivated and encouraging. Sharing your goals with someone helps you stay on track, provides accountability, and gives you a support system for when things get tough. Just like how football teams need their coaches to drive them forward, you need a coach to help keep your eye on the end goal.

When I started setting big goals, I learned the importance of keeping them in front of me, almost like a playbook. I loved writing, so I would jot down my goals and the steps I wanted to take to achieve them. At the top of my list was the goal of becoming an officer. I filled my dorm room with reminders—posters, quotes, and anything related to my vision. Those visuals kept me motivated daily, just like seeing your team's logo on the field reminds you of what you're working for.

> SMALL GOALS, LIKE FIRST DOWNS, BUILD MOMENTUM; BEFORE YOU KNOW IT, YOU'RE SCORING THE TOUCHDOWN.

A key strategy in reaching your goals is setting deadlines for each step. Think of it as aiming for a first down on the field. If you keep making those smaller gains, you'll eventually make it to the end zone. Small goals, like first downs, build momentum; before you know it, you're scoring the touchdown. Setting deadlines and breaking goals into smaller steps helps you avoid procrastination and keeps you focused.

But, like any good play, sometimes things don't go as planned. Everyone can't win all the time. Obstacles can come up, and you may have to adjust. Maybe you're injured, like I was, or face another setback. In those moments, you don't throw in the towel. Like in a game, you make a strategic pivot, call a new play, and keep moving toward the goal line. **A delay doesn't mean defeat**. It just means you might need a different approach or more time.

When my military career was cut short, I had to return to my playbook and reevaluate my path. I leaned on my coaches—family and friends—who reminded me of the skills I'd gained and helped me see new possibilities. My path changed, but I could transition into a new career with more confidence and purpose because I had a clear vision. Each step toward my original goal wasn't wasted; instead, it fueled my success in a different direction.

||||||||||||||||||||||||||||||||||||||||||||||||||||||||||||||||||||||||||||||||||||

Coaching Tip: Challenge yourself to find your own "coach"—someone who will help you stay on task, motivate you when things get tough, and celebrate with you when you reach your goals. With a clear vision, a robust support system, and a game plan, you'll be ready to tackle whatever comes your way.

||||||||||||||||||||||||||||||||||||||||||||||||||||||||||||||||||||||||||||||||||||

Write down the name of someone you trust who could coach you—someone who can support, guide, and keep you accountable on your journey. Within the next week, reach out to them. Share your vision, tell them about your goals, and ask if they'd be willing to help you stay on track.

My coach will be: _____

Dream Big

Reflecting on my journey, I can see how setting goals and pursuing my education opened doors I never imagined. Being the first in my family to graduate college wasn't just a milestone—it was the foundation that has continued to support and shape my life. I started dreaming of this goal during my junior year of high school. Although I wasn't the top student, I found ways to discipline myself, learn how to study, and push through challenges. I encountered setbacks and moments of doubt, but I kept moving forward, determined to reach that finish line.

Earning my degree wasn't the end of the journey—it was the beginning of a new world of opportunities. That degree unlocked paths I didn't even know were possible. I obtained my master's degree in public administration and a certificate in business administration from Keller Graduate School of Business. Now, as a business owner, I'm still reaping the benefits of the education for which I worked so hard. It's not just about career advancement. My education has allowed me to serve others, provide for my family, and create a meaningful life. It's a gift that keeps on giving, one that goes beyond me, extending to the people I work with, the students I mentor, and the community I love.

I hope my story encourages you to dream big and focus on your goals. Whether going to college, starting your own business, learning a trade, or giving back to your community, each step you take toward your dreams will add up. Remember, the journey isn't always easy. There will be times when you feel like giving up. But hold onto that vision. Find a coach, a friend, a family member, or a mentor who believes in you and can support you along the way. Let them help you, just as coaches guide their teams to victory.

You're writing your story right now as a winning leader. Every decision you make, every challenge you overcome, and every lesson you learn brings you closer to the life you're meant to live. Stay focused, stay determined, and remember that the journey is part of the reward. What you achieve is only the beginning—the impact you can make with it is limitless. So, take your dream seriously, commit to your goals, and know that each step forward brings you closer to a future full of potential and purpose.

Now, it's your turn. Dream big, work hard, and keep moving forward. The future is yours to shape.

Winning Leadership in Action

1. Working with a small group, pick three potential dream jobs or careers. Research the education, skills, and experiences needed to be successful in these jobs. Present your findings to the class to explore the connection between goals and required steps.
2. Create a two to three-minute "My Success" presentation. Describe your success story from the perspective of someone who has already achieved their vision. Describe what it took to get there, challenges overcome, and moments of triumph.

3. Write a letter to yourself ten years from now. In your letter, describe your dream and the steps you plan to take to achieve it. Seal the letter and keep it in a safe place. Open it up later to see how you have changed and assess how far you have come toward achieving your dreams.

4. Work with a partner to practice coaching each other. Review your partner's goals, offer encouragement, and suggest new ideas. At the end of your coaching session, talk together as a class about how you can support others as a "coach" in their journey.

THE DIRECTOR LEADERSHIP STYLE

Superpower of the Director Leader: Decisive Strategy

Pros and Cons of the Director Leadership Style

Pros of Being a Director	Examples in Action	Cons of Being a Director
Clear Vision and Direction—Directors have a strong sense of where they want to go and can map out a path to achieve it.	Setting a clear goal, such as "owning a welding business" or "working in health care," helps Directors stay focused.	Overly Controlling—Directors may be too focused on their way of doing things, potentially overlooking valuable input.
Goal-Oriented—Directors are driven to achieve objectives and often reach high levels of success.	Setting SMART goals, like applying to welding school, shows dedication to structured progress toward big dreams.	Difficulty Delegating—Directors might struggle to delegate tasks, thinking their way is best or fastest.

Pros of Being a Director	Examples in Action	Cons of Being a Director
Effective Problem-Solver— Directors tackle challenges head-on and look for solutions to overcome obstacles.	Setting specific deadlines, like for college applications, helps Directors meet milestones even when challenges arise.	May Struggle with Flexibility—Directors can be rigid and may struggle to adapt when plans take unexpected turns.
Confident Decision-Maker— Directors make timely decisions, providing clear direction and keeping projects on track.	Making prompt choices, such as applying to specific schools or internships, shows the confidence of a Director.	Can Appear Unapproachable—Strong decision-making can make a Director seem intimidating, discouraging others from input.

Tips for Thriving as a Director Leader

1. Encourage team input to enhance the quality of your decisions and show you value different perspectives.
2. Stay flexible by embracing a mindset that allows you to adjust plans when unexpected challenges arise.

3. Delegate wisely to foster teamwork, build trust, and avoid burnout.
4. Maintain approachability by practicing active listening and encouraging open dialogue so others feel valued and willing to contribute ideas.

Looking back on this step, what do you consider your most valuable takeaway? Write your answer below:

_____

_____

_____

_____

_____

_____

_____

_____

_____

_____

_____

_____

_____

_____

_____

_____

_____

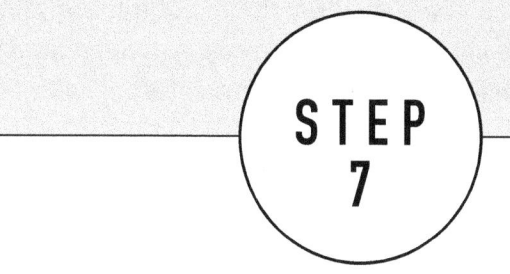

Serve to Be Great

Serving is the key to achieving greatness!

Servant Leadership

Imagine being a leader who inspires change by serving others, rolling up your sleeves, and making a difference. That's what servant leadership is all about. It is not about being the loudest or most recognized but about stepping up to serve others and leading by example. True greatness comes from helping those around you grow and succeed.

As you grow and develop as a winning leader, you are responsible for giving back to your community. Leadership isn't just about making decisions or giving directions—it's about using your skills, time, and influence to uplift and empower others. This is the heart of what Dr. Martin Luther King Jr. meant when he said everyone has the capacity for greatness through serving others. Serving isn't reserved for those in high-ranking positions or with significant resources. Anyone can do it regardless of background, economic status, talents, or circumstances.

True winning in leadership stems from the willingness to serve selflessly, placing the needs of others above your own. Whether helping a classmate with a difficult project, volunteering at a community event, or starting a service initiative, your ability to make a difference lies in your choice to serve. The most impactful leaders understand that their title or power does not measure their greatness. Their greatness is measured by the lives they touch and the positive changes they inspire through service. Every act of kindness, no matter how small, contributes to building a legacy of compassion and strength, proving that service is the cornerstone of exceptional leadership.

Leaders who serve understand their communities and take action to make them better. They tackle important issues, from homelessness and bullying to creating cleaner environments or promoting education. Ask yourself: What's important to me? What cause or need stirs my heart? Is it helping people experiencing homelessness, supporting cancer research, or creating a safe space for classmates? Search your heart to find what's important to you.

Start small—look around your school, neighborhood, or local community. Once you've made an impact there, you can expand your efforts outward.

Why Service Matters

Service is a critical component of becoming a winning leader. Giving back strengthens your community and helps those in need, creating a chain reaction of positive change. The best leaders almost always adopt the mindset of a servant, understanding that authentic leadership is about lifting others and helping them reach their full potential.

What makes leaders genuinely great is their ability to serve selflessly and inspire greatness in those around them. When you serve, you inspire others to do the same, creating a ripple effect that impacts more people than you could imagine. This energy can shift a school or campus culture or uplift an entire community.

Throughout history, many great leaders have embodied a servant's mindset, using their influential positions to uplift others and inspire meaningful change. Mahatma Gandhi, for example, led India's nonviolent movement for independence from British rule by prioritizing service, fostering peace, and sacrificing personal comfort for the greater good. His life was a testament to the power of humility and dedication to a cause bigger than oneself.

Mother Teresa dedicated her life to serving the poor and sick through the Missionaries of Charity in India. Her tireless efforts to provide care and compassion to society's most vulnerable transformed countless lives and inspired others worldwide to follow her example of selfless service.

Abraham Lincoln, the sixteenth president of the United States, demonstrated servant leadership during the Civil War, one of the nation's darkest periods. He placed the well-being of the country above personal power, striving to preserve the Union and abolish slavery. His unwavering commitment to justice and equality continues to serve as a model of ethical and empathetic leadership.

These leaders remind us that greatness is not about status or authority—it's about using your talents and influence to serve others and create a lasting impact. Their examples show that the most meaningful change often begins with a willingness to lead through service and inspire future generations to do the same.

The Ripple Effect of Service

So, how can you serve those in your community? Start small—lend a helping hand to a friend, join a volunteer project, or identify a need you can help address. When you act, it doesn't just change your life—it inspires others to join. Service has a ripple effect. It is almost like having a long row of dominoes. One small act of kindness or leadership leads to another. As others see your positive impact, they'll also be encouraged to get involved. This ripple effect builds a culture of service and collaboration that spreads throughout your school, community, and beyond.

By serving others, you're not just making a difference in the lives of those you help—you're setting the tone for a stronger, more united community. Over time, this mindset of giving back can transform the culture around you, creating an environment where kindness, leadership, and service thrive. Remember, every step you take to serve brings you closer to becoming a winning leader who inspires lasting change.

||||||||||||||||||||||||||||||||||||||||||||||||||||||||||||||||||||||||||||||||

Coaching Tip: Create a ripple effect in your community. Look around and identify one way you can make a difference this week. It could be as simple as helping a teacher organize supplies, tutoring a classmate, or starting a recycling initiative in the cafeteria. Take the lead by creating a plan, involving others if needed, and following through with action. After completing it, consider how it felt to serve and what impact it made.

||||||||||||||||||||||||||||||||||||||||||||||||||||||||||||||||||||||||||||||||

Examples of Servant Leaders

I know a coach at a major university who exemplifies servant leadership in the simplest yet most powerful way. Whenever he notices the floor needs mopping after practice, he doesn't wait for someone else to do it—he grabs the mop and gets to work. His actions speak volumes. As the team watches him take the initiative, they feel inspired to jump in and help. They think, *If the coach, our leader, is willing to do this, I should step up too.*

The coach sets a tone of humility and teamwork by leading through action. His willingness to serve creates a ripple effect, encouraging others to follow his example.

This is the essence of authentic leadership: modeling the behavior you want to see in others. When leaders roll up their sleeves and show they're not above any task, it fosters a culture where everyone is motivated to contribute. Service becomes contagious, and the entire team grows stronger because of it.

Consider how you could demonstrate a servant attitude in your job, no matter where you work. For example, if you're at a grocery store, start by being proactive and looking for ways to help others before they ask. Go above and beyond your assigned tasks and take initiative when you see something that needs to be done—even if it's not in your job description. If the trash needs taking out or a spill needs cleaning, step up and handle it without hesitation. Simple acts such as helping customers load groceries into their cars can make a big difference.

Being a team player is another way to show a servant's attitude. Support your coworkers by pitching in when they need help. If someone calls in sick, consider coming in early or staying late to cover for them. Treat everyone—coworkers, customers, and supervisors—courteously and professionally, regardless of their position. Active listening is critical, too. Pay close attention to what customers or team members say, anticipate their needs, and go the extra mile to make their experience positive. For instance, if a customer asks where to find something and you're unsure, don't just point them in the general direction—take the time to find the answer and guide them to it.

Reliability is a cornerstone of a servant's attitude. Be dependable, punctual, and consistent. When your employer sees that you can be trusted with small tasks, they'll feel confident assigning you more significant responsibilities. Ultimately, it's not just about completing tasks. Instead, it's about showing genuine enthusiasm for helping others and maintaining a positive, solutions-oriented attitude, even in challenging situations. That mindset will make you stand out and leave a lasting impression, creating a massive wave of change.

Service Learning

Volunteering is a two-way street: It helps others and helps you grow in unexpected ways. You develop valuable skills like communication, empathy, teamwork, and problem-solving when you serve. For example, when I volunteered at a local food bank, I learned how to organize tasks efficiently and communicate with a diverse group of people. Those skills later helped me take on leadership roles in school clubs and group projects.

Volunteering also teaches you about different experiences and challenges, helping you become a more compassionate and understanding leader. It changes the way you see the world and understand others. For instance, helping at a homeless shelter can teach you about the resilience of people who face challenging circumstances and show you the value of creating a welcoming environment. Similarly, participating in a community cleanup project might teach you the importance of teamwork and shared responsibility as you and others work toward a common goal. These experiences make you a better leader and help shape you into a more empathetic and thoughtful person.

Designing a Meaningful Service Project

You don't have to wait for someone else to take the lead—this is your chance to step up and create something meaningful. Designing a service project allows you to turn your passions into action while showing that you're a well-rounded person who genuinely cares about making a difference. Whether improving your school, helping your neighbors, or addressing a more significant community need, your efforts can leave a lasting impact.

Step 1: Identify a Need
- Look around your school, campus, neighborhood, or community to find issues that need attention (e.g., litter, hunger, outdated facilities).
- Talk to community leaders like a school principal, teachers, or business owners to understand specific needs.
- Think about what you care about most—helping classmates, supporting people without homes, or creating a cleaner environment.
- Example: Is there a playground that needs updating? Does a food bank need donations? Does a homeless shelter need a community garden?

Step 2: Pick a Project
- Choose something you're passionate about that aligns with the identified need.
- Example: Organize a food drive, start a community cleanup, or collect school supplies for classmates.

Step 3: Create a Plan

- **Set a Goal**: Be clear about what you want to achieve (e.g., collect 100 cans of food, clean up a local park).
- **Gather Supplies**: Identify what you'll need (e.g., trash bags, posters, collection bins).
- **Assign Roles**: Divide tasks among your team—someone can handle advertising, and others can focus on logistics.
- **Set a Timeline**: Create a schedule with deadlines to keep everything on track.
- **Example:** For a food drive, set up collection bins, create posters, and assign someone to count the donations.

Step 4: Act

- Execute your plan step by step. Stay organized and focused on your goals.
- Example: Advertise your project on social media, collect donations, and deliver them to the organization in need.

Step 5: Reflect on Your Work

- After the project, ask yourself and your team:
  - Did we meet our goals?
  - How did our efforts help others?
  - What challenges did we face, and how did we overcome them?
  - What lessons can we apply to future projects?
- Reflecting enables you to understand the impact of your work and grow as a leader.

- Example: "We collected 120 cans of food, exceeding our goal. Seeing how our small effort made a big difference in the community felt amazing."

Quick Tips for Service Success

Start small and grow as you gain experience. You might not be able to complete the entire project, but you might be able to do part of it.

- Set clear, measurable, and realistic goals to ensure your project is achievable.
- Involve others to make a more significant impact. The resources you discover when you team up with others are fantastic.
- Stay adaptable and remember that things may go differently than planned, but problem-solving is part of leadership.
- Celebrate your successes and share what you learned with others.

By following these steps, you'll create a service project that's not only meaningful but also a reflection of your leadership and commitment to making a difference.

Imagine Service in Your Future

Think about how you can weave service into your school, career, college life, and personal goals. Volunteering and serving others is not limited to one-time projects. Instead, it's a mindset you can carry into everything you do. What causes align with your passions and values? Whether helping children, protecting the environment, or supporting your community, service can become a meaningful part of your journey.

Consider how this mindset can shape your career. If you become a teacher, you'll serve students by guiding them toward their potential. As a nurse, you'll provide care and compassion to those in need. Entrepreneurs serve their communities by creating opportunities and solving problems. Whatever path you choose, a heart of service will make you a more decisive leader and a better person.

Small acts of service can lead to significant change. It starts with one individual at a time. Although you may only sometimes see the immediate impact, every effort counts. Helping one person can create a ripple effect, inspiring others to step up and make a difference.

Service is about looking beyond yourself and focusing on the greater good. When you bring people together to meet needs or solve problems, you create a culture of generosity and collaboration. More people will join and connect with the mission as your efforts grow. That's how the impact becomes sustainable and spreads.

Remember, the ripple effect starts with you. Whether a small act of kindness or a larger project, your actions can inspire others and build momentum. Serve and impact as many people as possible, and watch your contributions create lasting change in your community.

Go Out and Serve

Don't wait for opportunities to come your way—go out and create them. By serving others, you're not only helping your community, but you're also building yourself into a more decisive, more empathetic leader. A heart for service is the most important of all the leadership styles and skills you can develop.

Go out and do something great today. What will your first step be? Will you lend a hand to a classmate, organize a project, or support a cause that matters to you? Remember: no act of service is too small. It's the starting point for greatness.

Winning Leadership in Action

1. Search the internet for real-life stories of students making a difference through service. Share your findings with the class. Discuss what motivated them and how their actions inspired others.
2. Write a letter of thanks to someone who has served or helped you. Share how their actions inspired you to be a better leader.
3. Create a visual representation, such as a poster or drawings, to show how small acts of service can have a ripple effect and inspire change.
4. Working in small groups, brainstorm potential service projects your class or group could realistically

implement, such as tutoring peers, organizing a recycling program, or assisting a teacher. Once your group has brainstormed ideas, select one project to develop further. Create a basic plan for your project using the steps outlined in this chapter. Document your ideas on a large paper or poster board and share them with the class. Each group will present its project idea to the class when the brainstorming session ends. Explain how your project aligns with community values like compassion, inclusivity, or environmental responsibility. Highlight your project's specific benefits to the community and those involved in the effort. After all groups have shared their ideas, the class will vote on one project to adopt and collaborate on as an actual service initiative.

THE SERVER LEADERSHIP STYLE

Superpower of the Server Leader: Insightful Visionary

Pros and Cons of the Server Leadership Style

Pros of Being a Server	Examples in Action	Cons of Being a Server
Builds trust and loyalty among team members.	Leading a community service project, such as organizing a food drive or volunteering at a local shelter.	Can sometimes prioritize others' needs to the point of neglecting personal well-being or boundaries.
Creates a positive and inclusive environment where everyone feels valued.	Mentoring younger peers in an after-school program and helping them develop confidence and skills.	May struggle with decision-making in situations where assertiveness is required.

Pros of Being a Server	Examples in Action	Cons of Being a Server
Inspires others through humility and a genuine desire to help.	Assisting classmates with homework or organizing a study group to ensure everyone succeeds.	Can be taken advantage of by those who see their helpfulness as a weakness.
Builds strong relationships by being empathetic and understanding.	Supporting a teammate who is struggling emotionally by listening and offering practical solutions.	May hesitate to step into the spotlight, even when their ideas or contributions deserve recognition.
Develops a culture of mutual support and collaboration, leading to team success.	Volunteering to take on extra tasks to help a group meet a deadline or complete a project successfully.	Can become overwhelmed or burnt out by consistently taking on too much responsibility for others.

Tips for Thriving as a Server Leader

1. Set boundaries by learning to say no to protect your well-being and avoid burning out.
2. Balance service with leadership by remembering that serving others doesn't mean you always have to be in charge.

3. Communicate clearly by letting your team know your limitations while still offering support.
4. Practice self-care, taking time to recharge and focus on your goals for maximum effectiveness.
5. Delegate and empower others to take ownership of tasks so you're not carrying the entire load alone.
6. Celebrate contributions by acknowledging and uplifting others while still giving yourself credit for the difference you make.

Looking back on this step, what do you consider your most valuable takeaway? Write your answer below:

_____

_____

_____

_____

_____

_____

_____

_____

_____

_____

_____

_____

_____

Execute to Win

You don't win based on your feelings—you win through preparation, effort, and execution!

The Power of Execution

Execution is the final step in turning your winning leadership potential into action. It's where vision meets reality and effort produces results. Now is the time to take everything you've learned and put it into practice. Winning leadership isn't just about having ideas or goals; it's about following through. Winning doesn't happen by chance—it is the result of intentional preparation, focused effort, and flawless execution.

Great leaders embrace a growth mindset and commit to becoming lifelong learners. They see challenges not as obstacles but as opportunities to grow, adapt, and refine their abilities. Instead of fearing failure, they recognize it as a valuable teacher, learning from their mistakes and using these lessons to propel themselves forward. They understand that personal and professional growth comes through consistent effort and persistence, knowing that every step forward strengthens their potential.

Moreover, many great leaders actively seek feedback from others—whether it's peers, teachers, mentors, or members of their community. They understand that constructive criticism provides insights that they might not see on their own, helping them to improve and broaden their perspective. By embracing these practices, they not only sharpen their skills but also build relationships and foster collaboration—essential qualities for effective leadership.

This final step is about putting those strengths into action, refining your weaknesses, and being relentless in your growth. Winning leadership is an ongoing process, and the world is counting on you to lead with purpose, adaptability, and empathy.

Whether your strengths lie as a connector, server, influencer, or protector, or in another winning leadership style, great leaders know how to integrate all their skills to maximize their impact. Winning leadership isn't about being one-dimensional; it's about recognizing your natural strengths while continuously striving to develop in other areas. For example, you might excel as an observer, carefully analyzing situations and making thoughtful decisions, but to be a well-rounded leader, you also need to strengthen your director skills by learning how to take charge and execute plans effectively.

Becoming a winning leader is a lifelong journey of growth and self-improvement. It takes practice, reflection, and resilience to refine your abilities. Each winning leadership style offers unique qualities that can help you inspire and guide others. By embracing all aspects of leadership and stepping outside your comfort zone, you'll discover new opportunities to lead and serve with greater confidence and purpose. Leadership isn't a destination—it's a continuous process of learning, adapting, and striving to be your best self.

Embrace a Growth Mindset

Our world is continually changing, and winning leaders must develop a growth mindset to navigate these changes effectively. A prime example of a growth mindset in action is how the pandemic transformed our relationship with technology. Teachers who had spent their careers teaching in traditional classroom settings suddenly had to pivot to virtual learning almost overnight. They quickly adapted to using platforms like Zoom and Microsoft Teams for online classes and meetings, learning new tools and techniques to engage their students remotely. This shift required not only technical skills but also resilience, creativity, and willingness to embrace change.

The business world has undergone a profound digital transformation, particularly in response to challenges brought on by the pandemic. Consider how companies like Walmart adapted quickly to shifting consumer needs by expanding self-checkout lanes and enhancing online shopping platforms. These changes not only streamlined the shopping experience but also highlighted the growing importance of technology in everyday business operations. The pandemic accelerated trends that were already underway, demonstrating how vital it is for businesses to innovate and adapt to meet evolving demands.

Similarly, leaders in every field must be prepared to adapt when faced with unexpected challenges. Whether it's navigating a shift in workplace dynamics, responding to economic changes, or managing global disruptions, the ability to pivot and find solutions is essential. Adapting doesn't just mean finding a quick fix—it means embracing change as an opportunity for growth and innovation. Winning leaders who develop this mindset inspire confidence in others, demonstrate resilience, and create pathways for progress, even in the face of uncertainty. The pandemic taught us that those who embrace a growth mindset are better equipped to lead in a rapidly changing world.

Winning leaders never stop learning. You have to be prepared for change ahead. One thing is certain about the future: it will be ever-changing. Developing a growth mindset means embracing challenges as opportunities to grow and learning from mistakes. As you encounter setbacks or difficulties, ask yourself, *What can I learn from this?* Use those lessons to push forward.

Commit to lifelong learning. Take online courses, seek mentorship, read books, and stay curious. Growth-minded leaders know the value of keeping their skills sharp in an ever-changing world.

||||||||||||||||||||||||||||||||||||||||||||||||||||||||||||||||||||||||||||||||||||||||

Coaching Tip: Challenge yourself to write down one action you took that brought you closer to your goal and one lesson you learned. Reflect on how these align with the Eight Winning Steps. Share with a peer or mentor to gain new insights.

||||||||||||||||||||||||||||||||||||||||||||||||||||||||||||||||||||||||||||||||||||||||

Persevere Through Challenges

As a winning leader, there will be times when the path is hard and setbacks feel overwhelming. What defines you is how you handle those moments. During my early years in business, I didn't make a lot of money. In fact, it took almost four-and-a-half years before I started to see any money coming in from my business. It was often difficult to pay the bills, so I had to put off buying many things our family wanted in order to pursue our bigger dream of building a business. But this was a sacrifice that my wife and I were willing to make because we believed in what we had to offer and saw the value in it.

Despite sometimes wanting to quit, I stayed committed to my dream. That perseverance eventually paid off, both financially and personally. Eventually, opportunities came that allowed us to build and make more money.

Remember, setbacks are temporary. You will never achieve your dreams if you give up. Learn from your mistakes, adjust your plan, and keep moving forward.

Celebrate Progress

Celebrate the small wins on your path to success. Winning leadership isn't just about achieving big goals; it's about recognizing the steps that get you there.

For instance, if you improve your biology grade from a C to a B, celebrate that progress before aiming for a A. Take one step at a time, realizing that small steps lead to big successes. Acknowledging progress keeps you motivated and focused on your larger goals.

Regularly assess your growth so you can celebrate the progress and accomplishments of your journey. What did you accomplish this semester? What did you learn from the challenges? Fostering a mindset of celebrating accomplishments is essential. Don't be so hard on yourself, saying I've got to do this or that. Those things are great, but the joy is in the journey. Goal setting and self-discipline are very important because they help you take ownership of your growth and development. You need to find the winning leader within yourself—not just the leader that your parents or teachers want you to be.

||||||||||||||||||||||||||||||||||||||||||||||||||||||||||||||||||||||||||||||||

Coaching Tip: Don't wait until the finish line to celebrate! Take time to

recognize your progress, whether it's improving a grade, completing a challenging task, or overcoming a personal hurdle. Write down three accomplishments each week, no matter how small they may seem. Remember: small victories pave the way for big achievements!

||||||||||||||||||||||||||||||||||||||||||||||||||||||||||||||||||||||||||||||||||

The Winning Leadership Takeaway

If there's one message I want you to take away from this book, it's this: You are a winning leader, and the world needs your greatness. Inside you lies the power to win—the confidence, skills, talents, and abilities to lead and make a difference. The world needs your unique strengths to inspire change and positively impact the lives of others. Leadership isn't just about holding a title or being in the spotlight; it's about using what you have to serve, uplift, and guide those around you.

YOU ARE A WINNING LEADER, AND THE WORLD NEEDS YOUR GREATNESS.

You already have skills and qualities that set you apart, but as a winning leader, there is always room to grow. Ask yourself: How can I develop further? How can I add value to my life and to the lives of others? Winning leadership is about constant evolution—becoming better at what you do and helping others reach their full potential along the way.

Finding your voice is a crucial part of this journey. Maybe you're a quiet observer, analyzing situations and understanding people deeply. Maybe you're a natural influencer, inspiring others with your enthusiasm and energy. Whatever your style, your voice matters. The world faces countless challenges, from local community issues to global concerns. Each of us has a role to play in addressing these challenges—whether by serving, volunteering, or building connections within our communities.

Winning leadership is about stepping up and acting, no matter how big or small the task. It's about finding others who share your passions and working together to make a difference. When you think of yourself as a winning leader, you unlock the potential to create real change. Transformation happens when you take ownership of your leadership and encourage others to do the same.

Every skill you gain, every experience you encounter, and every obstacle you overcome contributes to your winning leadership journey. Winning leadership isn't reserved for the loudest voice or the most popular person—it's about using what you have and making an impact. It's about showing up, serving, and acting with purpose. Only when each of us does our part can we hope to make the world a better place.

So, embrace your role as a winning leader. Use your voice, act, and commit to growing and serving. The future needs your unique vision, and you have everything it takes to rise to the challenge. Your journey is just beginning—go out and make your mark on the world.

Your Final Charge

As you finish this book, take a moment to reflect on the kind of winning leader you want to become. Winning leadership isn't about perfection—it's about growth, effort, and action. Think about how you can use the **Eight Winning Leadership Steps** to create a meaningful impact in your life and the lives of others. Each step builds on the last, forming a roadmap to help you develop into a confident, purpose-driven leader.

Discover Your Strengths

What are your natural gifts and talents? How can you use them to make an impact in your school, family, or community? Recognizing your unique abilities is the foundation of effective leadership. Your strengths, combined with a clear vision, will set you apart as a leader who knows how to make things happen.

Observe and Listen

Take the time to truly see and hear the world around you. What needs are being overlooked? Whose voices are not being heard? Observant leaders are empathetic leaders—they find ways to address challenges and create solutions that matter.

Protect and Advocate

Stand up for what's right, even when it's not the popular choice. Advocate for those who need support, and use your voice to defend causes that align with your values. Being a Protector means having the courage to lead with integrity and compassion.

Connect with Others

Strong relationships are at the heart of winning leadership. Build connections with people who share your goals, values, and passions. Collaboration and trust are essential for achieving big things, whether it's organizing a community project or leading a team.

Learn and Grow

Winning leadership is a journey of lifelong learning. Commit to improving yourself by seeking feedback, developing new skills, and staying open to change. Challenges are opportunities to grow stronger and smarter—embrace them.

Dream Big

Don't be afraid to dream big, but remember, dreams require action. Set SMART goals that turn your vision into reality. Break those goals into steps and tackle them one by one. Success comes from consistent effort and determination.

Serve with Purpose

Lead by example. Serve your community, your peers, and those who look up to you. True leaders inspire others to follow their example, creating a ripple effect of positive change. How can you use your time and resources to uplift others and make a difference?

Execute to Win

The final step is about acting and staying resilient. Life will throw challenges your way, but great leaders adapt, persevere, and keep going. Winning doesn't happen by accident—it happens through preparation, focus, and execution.

As you move forward, revisit the **Eight Winning Leadership Steps** often. Reflect on how you can use them to guide your decisions and shape your actions. Winning leadership is not a one-time achievement—it's a lifelong commitment to learning, growing, and serving.

The world needs leaders like you. You have everything you need to make an impact: your unique strengths, your voice, and your determination. Now, it's up to you to step up, act, and become the winning leader you were always meant to be. Go out and make a difference—the world is waiting for you!

You Are Ready

The game is on, and the world is waiting for your voice, your leadership, and your unique perspective. As your coach, I've shared the plays, strategies, and winning steps to help you succeed. Now, it's time to take the field and put them into action.

Lead with confidence. Serve with humility. Execute your vision with purpose. Remember: just like in the biggest games, you don't win on emotion—you win on preparation, discipline, and execution.

Every decision you make and every action you take has the power to create positive change. You've got the skills, the mindset, and the drive to make an impact. Believe in yourself and lead the way.

Let's go out there and make this world a better place— one decision, one action, and one winning leader at a time. I'm rooting for you every step of the way.

Congratulations on accepting **The Winning Leadership Challenge**. Now Let's Go Win Today!

Coach Kelly

Winning Leadership in Action

1. Work together in groups of three to five for the **Perseverance Tower Challenge** and see who can build the tallest free-standing structure! You'll have twenty minutes to create a tower using only twenty marshmallows, thirty toothpicks, and a small paper cup. The goal is for your tower to support the cup at the top without tipping over. After the challenge, take time to reflect as a group on what the experience taught you about perseverance, teamwork, and adapting to unexpected challenges.

2. Work with your team to design a fun and creative game that teaches others about having a growth mindset. For example, you could create a bingo game with growth mindset activities like "Tried something new," "Helped a friend solve a problem," or "Kept going after a failure." Or, you might design a board game where players overcome challenges and learn valuable lessons about perseverance and growth along the way. Use your creativity to come up with a unique and exciting game that will inspire others to embrace challenges, learn from mistakes, and grow into their best selves!

3. Read a chapter from a leadership-focused book and discuss how its lessons apply to your life. Share what you learned from your reading with a friend.

4. Pair up with a classmate and take turns being the coach and the player. As the coach, your goal is

to help your partner work through a challenge by asking thoughtful questions, practicing active listening, and offering constructive feedback. Encourage your partner to think about their strengths, identify possible solutions, and outline the next steps in their leadership journey. When you switch roles, reflect on what it felt like to guide someone else and to receive coaching. After the activity, discuss as a class how being both a coach and a player can help you grow as a winning leader.

Looking back on this step, what do you consider your most valuable takeaway? Write your answer below:

_____

_____

_____

_____

_____

_____

_____

_____

_____

_____

_____

_____

_____

ABOUT THE AUTHOR

KELLY SIMMONS III—BETTER known as Coach Kelly—was born and raised in Anderson, South Carolina. A first-generation college graduate from Lander University, he served as a US Army officer before medically retiring due to injury. After his military service, Coach Kelly transitioned into corporate sales and then discovered his true calling in education.

Over the past fifteen years , he has worked as a career counselor at a charter high school, a job readiness coach, and an adjunct instructor in higher education. Through these experiences, Coach Kelly has found his purpose: serving and empowering students and young adults.

He fulfills his mission through his books, keynote speaking, educational workshops, and *The Winning Leadership Dept.*, a dynamic podcast he created to engage, educate, and empower the next generation of leaders. By helping them become confident, innovative, and ethical leaders in their personal lives, careers, and communities, Coach Kelly continues to make a lasting impact on emerging leaders everywhere as founder and CEO of Empowered To Win LLC.

For more empowerment, please subscribe and follow Coach Kelly:
Instagram @coachkellysimmons
YouTube @coachkellysimmons
LinkedIn: Kelly Simmons III "Coach Kelly"
Website: coachkellysimmons.com

To implement **The Winning Leadership Challenge** in your school, organization, or community, contact Coach Kelly today. As a sought-after student empowerment speaker and leadership trainer, he can speak at your youth conference, assembly, even or facilitate a breakout session or provide professional development for your staff—equipping them with the tools to succeed and thrive as future leaders.
Email: admin@coachkellysimmons.com

If you found **The Winning Leadership Challenge** to be a helpful resource for you or any student you know, be sure to leave a positive review on Amazon. Thank you!

www.ingramcontent.com/pod-product-compliance
Lightning Source LLC
Chambersburg PA
CBHW061757120626
46550CB00005B/2032